Meeting SEN
in the Curriculum:
MUSIC

Other titles in the Meeting SEN in the Curriculum series:

Meeting Special Needs in English
Tim Hurst
1 84312 157 3

Meeting Special Needs in Maths
Brian Sharp
1 84312 158 1

Meeting Special Needs in Modern Foreign Languages
Sally McKeown
1 84312 165 4

Meeting Special Needs in Religious Education
Dilwyn Hunt
1 84312 167 0

Meeting Special Needs in History
Richard Harris and Ian Luff
1 84312 163 8

Meeting Special Needs in Design and Technology
Louise Davies
1 84312 166 2

Meeting Special Needs in Art
Kim Earle and Gill Curry
1 84312 161 1

Meeting Special Needs in PE and Sport
Crispin Andrews
1 84312 164 6

Meeting Special Needs in ICT
Mike North and Sally McKeown
1 84312 160 3

Meeting Special Needs in Science
Carol Holden
1 84312 159 X

Meeting Special Needs in Geography
Diane Swift
1 84312 162 X

Meeting Special Needs in Citizenship
Alan Combes
1 84312 169 7

Meeting SEN
in the Curriculum:
MUSIC

Victoria Jaquiss and Diane Paterson

David Fulton Publishers

David Fulton Publishers Ltd
The Chiswick Centre, 414 Chiswick High Road, London W4 5TF

www.fultonpublishers.co.uk

First published in Great Britain by David Fulton Publishers

10 9 8 7 6 5 4 3 2 1

David Fulton Publishers is a division of Granada Learning, part of ITV plc.

British Library Cataloguing in Publication Data
A catalogue record for this book is available from the British Library.

ISBN 1 84312 168 9

Typeset by Servis Filmsetting Ltd, Manchester
Printed and bound in Great Britain

Contents

Foreword

For the last 18 years or so I have been involved in music making with groups of young people many of whom have had special needs. If we had been doing gymnastics or football the whole exercise might have served only to point up the differences between the disabled and the non-disabled, but music can be made accessible to everyone. So by using music as a lubricant we have been able to create fantastic teams of young people working on an equal footing and put on performances that have amazed people and delighted the performers themselves.

It seems quite obvious that if you educate young people in subjects that they enjoy and succeed at, it will be easier later to slip in the vital stuff with less chance of rejection.

This book is a vital part of this process. Music can bring joy to everyone, and make the challenging business of secondary education more joyful than it sometimes seems to be.

RICHARD STILGOE
April 2005

Acknowledgements

The authors and publishers would like to thank:

- Mavis West and Jan Holdstock for their inspiration and experience.

- All their friends at YAMSEN (The Yorkshire Association for Music and Special Educational Needs), especially the late Gordon Parry, for their support, encouragement and belief.

- Charlotte Emery for her pictures.

- All those pupils and teachers in Leeds who we worked with.

- Bob Spooner for his belief in Victoria.

- The Drake Music Project for teaching Diane the ropes of enabling music technology.

- Colin Brackley-Jones for creating our working partnership.

- Sally Zimmerman and the RNIB for advice and encouragement for Diane.

- Mick Pitchford for inspirational training.

- Catherine J. Stockdale for kick-starting us.

- Lee Boyes for keeping us going when we started to droop.

- Anne Hewitt for her tireless support and reading the original draft.

- Karen Ruzicka, Sheila Hardwick and Yvonne Smith for their advice.

- Natalie, Xanthe, and Janet for sharing their ideas.

- Both our families for their patience in the face of neglect.

- Rick for his continuous support and cooking.

Contributors to the Series

The authors

Victoria Jaquiss took her Russian degree, teacher-trained in English and Drama, and taught English, PSE and just about everything else at Foxwood School, Leeds from 1980 till 1996, by which time she had become Head of Music and Expressive Arts. Since then she has been steel pan development officer for Leeds, and the SEN specialist for music for children with emotional and behavioural difficulties. She devised a system of musical notation primarily for use with steel pans, for which, in 2002, she was awarded the fellowship of the Royal Society of Arts.

Diane Paterson works as an Inclusive Music Curriculum Teacher in Leeds. In her spare time she volunteers with the charity Yorkshire Association for Music and Special Educational Needs. Diane has seven years' experience as a secondary school teacher. She has taught a WEA musical appreciation class to adults with brain injury and following this became a tutor with the Drake Music Project, exploring ways of enabling musicians who were disabled to make music using new technologies. In 1996 Diane took up a post with Leeds Music Support Service teaching music to children with special educational needs.

Series editor

Alan Combes started teaching in South Yorkshire in 1967 and was Head of English at several secondary schools before taking on the role of Head of PSHE as part of being senior teacher at Pindar School, Scarborough. He took early retirement to focus on his writing career and has authored two citizenship text books as well as writing several features for the TES. He has been used as an adviser on citizenship by the DfES and has emphasised citizenship's importance for special needs pupils as a speaker for NASEN.

A dedicated team of SEN specialists and subject specialists have contributed to the *Meeting Special Needs in the Curriculum* series.

SEN specialists

Sue Briggs is a freelance education consultant based in Hereford. She writes and speaks on inclusion, special educational needs and disability, and autistic spectrum disorders and is a lay member of the SEN and Disability Tribunal. Until recently, she was SEN Inclusion Co-ordinator for Herefordshire Education Directorate. Originally trained as a secondary music teacher, Sue has extensive experience in mainstream and special schools. For six years she was teacher in charge of a language disorder unit.

Sue Cunningham is a Learning Support Co-ordinator at a large mainstream secondary school in the West Midlands where she manages a large team of Learning Support teachers and assistants. She has experience of working in both mainstream and special schools and has set up and managed a Resource Base for Pupils with Moderate Learning Difficulties in the mainstream as part of an initiative to promote a more inclusive education for pupils with SEN.

Sally McKeown has held responsibility for language-based work in the Inclusion team at Becta. She has a particular interest in learning difficulties and dyslexia. She wrote the MFL Special Needs Materials for CILT's NOF training and is author of *Unlocking Potential* and co-author of *Supporting Children with Dyslexia* (Questions Publishing.) She writes regularly for the *TES, Guardian and Special Children* magazines.

Subject specialists

English

Tim Hurst has been a special educational needs co-ordinator in five schools and is particularly interested in the role and use of language in teaching.

Science

Carol Holden works as a science teacher and assistant SENCO in a mainstream secondary school. She has developed courses for pupils with SEN within science and has gained a graduate diploma and MA in Educational Studies, focusing on SEN.

Andy Cooke was a secondary science teacher for 14 years. He has been a KS3 Science co-ordinator, head of physics and head of science. He has experience of teaching visually impaired and is currently Science Adviser for Herefordshire. He is the author of the Spectrum series (Cambridge University Press).

History

Richard Harris has been teaching since 1989. He has taught in three comprehensive schools, as history teacher, Head of Department and Head of Faculty. He has also worked as teacher consultant for secondary history in West Berkshire.

Ian Luff is Assistant Head teacher of Kesgrave High School, Suffolk and has been Head of History in three comprehensive schools.

Maths

Brian Sharp Key Stage 3 Mathematics consultant for Herefordshire.
Brian has a long experience of working both in special and mainstream schools as a teacher of mathematics. He has a range of management experience, including SENCO, mathematics and ICT co-ordinator.

Religious education

Dilwyn Hunt has worked as a specialist RE adviser first in Birmingham and now in Dudley. He has a wide range of experience in the teaching of RE including mainstream and special RE.

Geography

Diane Swift is a project leader for the Geographical Association. Her interest in special needs developed whilst she was a Staffordshire geography adviser and inspector.

PE and sport

Crispin Andrews is an education/sports writer with nine years' experience of teaching and sports coaching.

Art

Kim Earle is Able Pupils Consultant for St Helens and has been a Head of Art and Design. Kim is also a practising designer jeweller.

Gill Curry is Gifted and Talented Strand Co-ordinator for the Wirral. She has twenty years' experience as Head of Art and has also been an Art Advisory Teacher. She is also a practising artist specialising in print.

Design and technology

Louise T. Davies is Principal Officer for Design and Technology at the Qualifications and Curriculum Authority, and also a freelance consultant. She is an experienced presenter and author of award winning resources and books for schools. She chairs the Special Needs Advisory Group for the Design and Technology Association.

ICT

Mike North works for ICTC, an independent consultancy specialising in the effective use of ICT in education. He develops educational materials and provides advice and support for the SEN sector.

Sally McKeown is an Education Officer with Becta, the government funded agency responsible for managing the National Grid for Learning and the FERL website. She is responsible for the use of IT for learners with disabilities, learning difficulties or additional needs.

Citizenship

Alan Combes started teaching in South Yorkshire in 1967 and was Head of English at several secondary schools before taking on the role of Head of PSHE as part of being senior teacher at Pindar School, Scarborough. He took early retirement to focus on his writing career and has authored two citizenship text-books as well as writing several features for the *TES*. He has been used as an adviser on citizenship by the DfES and has emphasised citizenship's importance for special needs pupils as a speaker for NASEN.

Modern foreign languages

Sally McKeown is responsible for language-based work in the Inclusion team at Becta. She has a particular interest in learning difficulties and dyslexia. She writes regularly for the *TES, Guardian* and *Special Children* magazine.

Contents of the CD

The CD contains basic record sheets, which can be adapted and personalised to suit you and your school, or used 'off the peg' as they are. Some have portrait and landscape styles, the latter for pupils who need more space to write. In some cases, pupils could be asked to choose which alternative is best for them. The sheets can be enlarged and colours added/changed for ease of reading; they can be put onto the student's own individual computer.

1. Inclusive Music Room Rules

2. Music Questionnaire

3. Record of Performance

4. Record of Attendance

5. Record of Concerts

6. Record of Songs and Instruments Learnt

7. Record of Attendance at Rehearsals

8. Individual Behaviour Plan (blank and sample)

9. Composition Grid

10. Targets/Switch Review Sheet

11. Record of lessons

12. Inclusive Checklists for TAs in Music

13. Inclusive Lesson plan (blank)

14. Dos and Don'ts for Good Behaviour

15. INSET Activity

16. Sample Policy

17. Sample Worksheets

18. Case Studies

19. Foxwood Listening Sheet

We would like to dedicate this book to the memory of:

Diane's husband, Stuart, whose untimely illness and death taught her the significance of using music to reach people;

and to all the wonderful staff at the late Foxwood School and all the families of Seacroft upon whose children Victoria practised what she now preaches.

Introduction

All children have the right to a good education and the opportunity to fulfil their potential. All teachers should expect to teach children with special educational needs (SEN) and all schools should play their part in educating children from the local community, whatever their background or ability. (*Removing Barriers to Achievement: The Government's Strategy for SEN*, Feb. 2004.)

A raft of legislation and statutory guidance over the past few years has sought to make our mainstream education system more inclusive and ensure that pupils with a diverse range of ability and need are well catered for. This means that all staff, including teachers of music need to have an awareness of how children learn and develop in different ways and an understanding of how barriers to achievement can be removed – or at least minimised.

These barriers often result from inappropriate teaching styles, inaccessible teaching materials or ill-advised grouping of pupils, as much as from an individual child's physical, sensory or cognitive impairments: a fact which is becoming better understood. It is this developing understanding that is now shaping the legislative and advisory landscape of our education system, and exhorting all teachers to carefully consider their curriculum planning and classroom practice.

Teachers of music in mainstream schools can expect to meet pupils with a wide range of individual needs and are well positioned to be able to meet those needs and ensure access to the music curriculum. Music also offers students a medium in which they can develop a range of important skills and attributes:

- listening skills

- improved concentration and attention to detail

- opportunities for rehearsing and over-learning

- fine motor control skills

- performance skills – and the raised self-esteem that performing can bring

As a subject on the school timetable, music can also appeal to many pupils with special needs by virtue of its 'hands-on' nature and the relatively small requirement for writing. It is an area where students can succeed when seeming to be a failure in other subjects and it offers perfect opportunities for working together in ensemble work in an environment where everyone has something to offer. For this to happen, however, the music teacher needs to have an understanding of the nature of the problems encountered by pupils and an armoury of approaches and resources to meet particular needs. This book sets out to help provide the information and guidance which will ensure that teachers of music have the knowledge and skills to make effective provision for students with SEN. It has been written by subject specialists with support from colleagues who have expertise within the SEN field so that the information and guidance given is both subject specific and pedagogically sound. The two main writers have over 50 years of teaching experience between them, mostly in the field of music, from early years to adult education, in mainstream and special settings, in the inner city and the leafy lanes.

The major statutory requirements and non-statutory guidance are summarised in Chapter 1, setting the context for this resource and providing useful starting points for departmental Inset.

It is clear that provision for pupils with special educational needs is not the sole responsibility of the SENCO and her team of assistants. If, in the past, subject teachers have 'taken a back seat' in the planning and delivery of a suitable curriculum for these children and expected the Learning Support department to bridge the gap between what was on offer in the classroom or music studio and what they actually needed – they can no longer do so.

> All teaching and non teaching staff should be involved in the development of the school's SEN policy and be fully aware of the school's procedure for identifying, assessing and making provision for pupils with SEN.
>
> (Table of Roles and Responsibilities, Revised/DfES *Code of Practice* 2001)

Chapter 2 looks at departmental policy for SEN provision and provides useful audit material for reviewing and developing current practice.

The term 'special educational needs' or SEN is now widely used and has become something of a catch-all descriptor – rendering it less than useful in many cases. Before the Warnock Report (1978) and subsequent introduction of the term 'special educational needs', any pupils who for whatever reason (cognitive difficulties, emotional and behavioural difficulties, speech and language disorders) progressed more slowly than the 'norm' were designated 'remedials' and grouped together in the bottom sets, without the benefit, in many cases, of specialist subject teachers.

But the SEN tag was also applied to pupils in special schools who had more significant needs and had previously been identified as 'disabled' or even 'uneducable'. Add to these the deaf pupils, those with impaired vision, others with mobility problems, and even children from other countries, with a limited understanding of the English language – who may or may not have been highly intelligent – and you have a recipe for confusion to say the least.

The day-to-day descriptors used in the staffroom are gradually being moderated and refined as greater knowledge and awareness of special needs is built up. (We still hear staff describing pupils as 'totally thick', a 'nutcase' or 'complete moron' – but hopefully only as a means of letting off steam!) However, there are terms in common use which, though more measured and well-meaning, can still be unhelpful and misleading. Teachers will describe a child as being 'dyslexic' when they mean that he is poor at reading and writing; 'ADHD' has become a synonym for badly behaved, and a child who seems to be withdrawn or just eccentric is increasingly described as 'autistic'.

The whole process of applying labels is fraught with danger, but sharing a common vocabulary – and more importantly, a common understanding – can help colleagues to express their concerns about a pupil and address the issues as they appear in the music room. Often, this is better achieved by identifying the particular areas of difficulty experienced by the pupil rather than puzzling over what syndrome he may have. The Code of Practice identifies four main areas of difficulty and these are detailed in Chapter 3 – along with an 'at a glance' guide to a wide range of syndromes and conditions and guidance on how they might present barriers to learning.

There is no doubt that the number of children with special needs being educated in mainstream schools is growing:

> . . . because of the increased emphasis on the inclusion of children with SEN in mainstream schools the number of these children is increasing, as are the severity and variety of their SEN. Children with a far wider range of learning difficulties and variety of medical conditions, as well as sensory difficulties and physical disabilities, are now attending mainstream classes. The implication of this is that mainstream school teachers need to expand their knowledge and skills with regard to the needs of children with SEN. (Stakes and Hornby 2000:3)

The continuing move to greater inclusion means that all teachers can now expect to teach pupils with varied and quite significant special educational needs at some time. Even five years ago, it was rare to come across children with Asperger's/Down's/Tourette's Syndrome, Autistic Spectrum Disorder or significant physical/sensory disabilities in community secondary schools. Now, they are entering mainstream education in growing numbers and there is a realisation that their 'inclusion' cannot be simply the responsibility of the SENCO and support staff. All staff have to be aware of particular learning needs and able to employ strategies in music that directly address those needs.

Chapter 4 considers the components of an inclusive music room and how the physical environment and resources can make a real difference to pupils with special needs. Instruments and equipment are considered and advice is offered on how informed choices can enable teachers to help students make music. Chapter 5 looks more closely at teaching and learning styles and consider ways in which to help all pupils maximise their potential.

Performing to an audience can give pupils a tremendous amount of satisfaction and enjoyment – and have a real impact on their self-confidence. In Chapter 6, we consider the how, why, what and where of performance, followed by guidance to listening to music in Chapter 7.

The monitoring of pupils' progress is a key factor in identifying and meeting their learning needs. Those who make slower progress than their peers are often working just as hard, or even harder, but their efforts can go unrewarded. Chapter 8 addresses the importance of realistic expectations and subsequent assessment and review in acknowledging pupils' achievements.

Liaising with the Special Educational Needs Co-ordinator (SENCO) and support staff is an important part of every teacher's role. The SENCO's status in a secondary school often means that she is part of the leadership team and influential in shaping whole school policy and practice; specific duties might include

- ensuring liaison with parents and other professionals

- advising and supporting teaching and support staff

- ensuring that appropriate Individual Education Plans are in place

- ensuring that relevant background information about individual children with special educational needs is collected, recorded and updated

- making plans for future support and setting targets for improvement

- monitoring and reviewing action taken

The SENCO has invariably undergone training in different aspects of special needs provision and has much to offer colleagues in terms of in-house training and advice about appropriate materials to use with pupils. She should be a frequent and valuable point of reference for all staff, but is often overlooked in this capacity. Her presence at the occasional departmental meeting can be very effective in developing teachers' skills in relation to meeting SEN, making them aware of new initiatives and methodology and sharing information about individual children.

In most schools however, the SENCO's skills and knowledge are channelled to the chalkface via a team of teaching or learning support assistants (TAs, LSAs). These assistants can be very able and well-qualified, but very underused in the classroom. Chapter 9 looks at how music teachers can manage Teaching Assistants in a way that makes the best use of a valuable resource.

Chapter 10 serves as a summary of the principles involved in providing for students with special needs in music.

The revised regulations for SEN provision make it clear that mainstream schools are expected to provide for pupils with a wide diversity of needs, and teaching is evaluated on the extent to which all pupils are engaged and enabled to achieve. This book has been produced in response to the implications of all of this for secondary subject teachers. The book and accompanying CD provide a resource that can be used with colleagues:

- to shape departmental policy and practice for special needs provision

- enable staff to react with a measured response when inclusion issues arise

- ensure that every pupil achieves appropriately and enjoys their music lessons.

CHAPTER 1

Meeting Special Educational Needs – Your Responsibility

Inclusion in education involves the process of increasing the participation of students in, and reducing their exclusion from, the cultures, curricula and communities of local schools. (*Index for Inclusion* 2000)

The *Index for Inclusion* was distributed to all maintained schools by the Department for Education and Skills and has been a valuable tool for many schools as they have worked to develop their inclusive practice. It supports schools in the review of their policies, practices and procedures, and the development of an inclusive approach, and where it has been used as part of the school improvement process – looking at inclusion in the widest sense – it has been a great success.

The *Index* demands that schools:

1. create a climate where everyone is valued

2. put inclusion at the heart of school development, permeating all policies

3. make school practices reflect the inclusive cultures and policies of the school.

For many people however, the Index lacked any real teeth and recent legislation and non-statutory guidance is more authoritative.

The SEN and Disability Act 2001 (SENDA)

The Act amended the Disability Discrimination Act 1995 and created important new duties for schools:

- to take reasonable steps to ensure that disabled pupils are not placed at a substantial disadvantage in relation to the education and other services they provide. This means they must anticipate where barriers to learning lie and take action to remove them as far as they are able

- to plan strategically to increase the extent to which disabled pupils can participate in the curriculum, make the physical environment more accessible and ensure that written material is provided in accessible formats

The reasonable steps taken might include:

- changing policies and practices

- changing course requirements

- changing physical features of a building

- providing interpreters or other support workers

- delivering courses in alternative ways

- providing materials in other formats and adapting musical instruments/equipment

(See Chapter 2 for further detail on SENDA and an INSET activity.)

The Revised National Curriculum

The Revised National Curriculum (2001) emphasises the provision of effective learning opportunities for all learners and establishes three principles for promoting inclusion:

- the setting of suitable learning challenges

- responding to pupils' diverse learning needs

- overcoming potential barriers to learning and assessment

The National Curriculum guidance suggests that music teachers may need to differentiate tasks and materials, and facilitate access to learning by:

- encouraging pupils to use all available senses and experiences

- planning for participation in all activities

- helping pupils to manage their behaviour, take part in learning and prepare for work

- helping pupils to manage their emotions

    - choosing material from earlier key stages, providing consideration is given to age-appropriate learning context. (This means that a fourteen-year-old with significant learning difficulties may be taught relevant aspects of the programmes of study for music at KS3 , but at the same time working on suitable material founded in the PoS for Key Stage 1.)

- maintaining and reinforcing previous learning, as well as introducing new knowledge, skills and understanding

- focusing on one aspect, or a limited number of aspects in depth or outline, of the age-related programmes of study

- clearly identifying the starting point for each aspect

- providing access to appropriate ICT to support and develop pupils' work at all key stages, for example, computer programs, switches, sound beams, communication aids, recording equipment. ICT provides many pupils with alternative ways to cause, create, choose, link and change sounds and music and help them take part as fully as possible in the music curriculum.

The Qualifications and Curriculum Authority (QCA) has also introduced performance descriptions (P levels/P scales) to enable teachers to observe and record small steps of progress made by some pupils with SEN. These descriptions outline early learning and attainment for each subject in the National Curriculum, including music. They chart progress up to NC level 1 through eight steps. The performance descriptions for P1 to P3 are common across all subjects and outline the types and range of general performance that some pupils with learning difficulties might characteristically demonstrate. From level P4, many believe it is possible to describe performance in a way that indicates the emergence of subject-focused skills, knowledge and understanding.

The Code of Practice for Special Educational Needs

The Revised Code of Practice (implemented in 2002) describes a cyclical process of planning, target setting and review for pupils with special educational needs. It also makes clear the expectation that the vast majority of pupils with special needs will be educated in mainstream settings. Those identified as needing over and above what the school can provide from its own resources, however, are nominated for 'School action plus', and outside agencies will be involved in

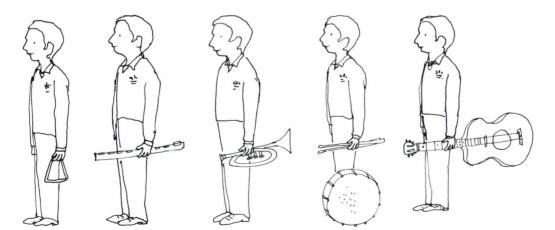

Inclusive provision may not look the same for all pupils

planned intervention. This may involve professionals from the Learning Support Service, a specialist teacher or therapist, or an educational psychologist, working with the school's Special Educational Needs Co-ordinator (SENCO) to put together an Individual Education Plan (IEP) for the pupil. In a minority of cases (the numbers vary widely between LEAs) pupils may be assessed by a multi-disciplinary team on behalf of the local education authority whose representatives then decide whether or not to issue a Statement of SEN. This is a legally binding document detailing the pupil's needs and setting out the resources which should be provided. It is reviewed every year.

FUNDAMENTAL PRINCIPLES OF THE SPECIAL NEEDS CODE OF PRACTICE:

- A pupil with special educational needs should have their needs met

- The special educational needs of pupils will normally be met in mainstream schools or settings

- The views of the pupil should be sought and taken into account

- Parents have a vital role to play in supporting their pupil's education

- Pupils with special educational needs should be offered full access to a broad, balanced and relevant education, including an appropriate curriculum for the foundation stage and the National Curriculum

---

Ofsted

Ofsted inspectors are required to make judgements about a school's inclusion policy, and how this is translated into practice in individual classrooms. According to Ofsted (2003) the following key factors help schools to become more inclusive:

- a climate of acceptance of all pupils

- careful preparation of placements for pupils with SEN

- availability of sufficient suitable teaching and personal support

- widespread awareness among staff of the particular needs of SEN pupils and an understanding of the practical ways of meeting these needs in the classroom

- sensitive allocation to teaching groups and careful curriculum modification, timetables and social arrangements

- availability of appropriate materials and teaching aids and adapted accommodation

- an active approach to personal and social development, as well as to learning

- well defined and consistently applied approaches to managing difficult behaviour

- assessment, recording and reporting procedures which can embrace and express adequately the progress of pupils with more complex SEN who make only small gains in learning

- involving parents/carers as fully as possible in decision-making, keeping them well informed about their pupil's progress and giving them as much practical support as possible

- developing and taking advantage of training opportunities, including links with special schools and other schools

Policy into practice

Effective teaching for pupils with special educational needs is by and large, effective for all pupils, but as schools become more inclusive, teachers need to be able to respond to a wider range of needs. The Government's strategy for SEN (*Removing Barriers to Learning*, (2004)) sets out ambitious proposals to 'help teachers expand their repertoire of inclusive skills and strategies and plan confidently to include pupils with increasingly complex needs'.

In many cases, pupils' individual needs will be met through greater differentiation of tasks and materials, i.e. school-based intervention as set out in the SEN Code of Practice (School Action). A smaller number of pupils may need access to specialist equipment and approaches or to alternative or adapted activities, as part of a 'school action plus' programme, augmented by advice and support from external specialists. The QCA give the following guidance on their website (2003):

Teachers are encouraged to take specific action to provide access to learning for pupils with special educational needs by:

(a) providing for pupils who need help with communication, language and literacy, through

- using texts that pupils can read and understand

- using visual and written materials in different formats, including large print, symbol text and Braille

- using ICT, other technological aids and taped materials

- using alternative and augmentative communication, including signs and symbols

- using translators, communicators and amanuenses

- using alternative notations, particularly in music

(b) planning, where necessary, to develop pupils' understanding through the use of all available senses and experiences

- using materials and resources that pupils can access through sight, touch, sound, taste or smell

- using word descriptions and other stimuli to make up for a lack of first-hand experiences

- using ICT, visual and other materials to increase pupils' knowledge of the wider world

- encouraging pupils to take part in everyday activities such as assemblies, concerts and class visits

(c) planning for pupils' full participation in learning and in physical and practical activities

- using specialist aids and equipment

- providing support from adults or peers when needed

- adapting tasks or environments

- providing alternative activities, where necessary

(d) helping pupils to manage their behaviour, to take part in learning effectively and safely, and, at Key Stage 4, to prepare for work

- setting realistic demands and stating them explicitly

- using positive behaviour management, including a clear structure of rewards and sanctions

- giving pupils every chance and encouragement to develop the skills they need to work well with a partner or a group

- teaching pupils to value and respect the contribution of others

- encouraging and teaching independent working skills

- teaching essential safety rules

(e) helping individuals to manage their emotions, particularly trauma or stress, and to take part in learning.

- identifying aspects of learning in which the pupil will engage and plan short-term, easily achievable goals in selected activities

- providing positive feedback to reinforce and encourage learning and build self-esteem

- selecting tasks and materials sensitively to avoid unnecessary stress for the pupil

- creating a supportive learning environment in which the pupil feels safe and is able to engage with learning

- allowing time for the pupil to engage with learning and gradually increasing the range of activities and demands

Pupils with disabilities

Not all pupils with disabilities will necessarily have special educational needs. Many learn alongside their peers with little need for additional resources beyond the aids which they use as part of their daily life, such as a wheelchair, a hearing aid or equipment to aid vision. Teachers' planning must ensure, however, that these pupils are enabled to participate as fully and effectively as possible in the curriculum by:

- planning appropriate amounts of time to allow for the satisfactory completion of tasks. This might involve:

  – taking account of the very slow pace at which some pupils will be able to record work, either manually or with specialist equipment, and of the physical effort required

  – being aware of the high levels of concentration necessary for some pupils when following or interpreting text or graphics, particularly when using vision aids or tactile methods, and of the tiredness which may result

  – allocating sufficient time, opportunity for pupils to experiment with new sound sources and instruments

  – being aware of the effort required by some pupils to follow aural/oral work, whether through use of residual hearing, lip reading or a signer, and of the tiredness or loss of concentration which may occur.

- planning opportunities, where necessary, for the development of skills in practical aspects of the curriculum. This might involve:

  – introducing new musical equipment (as explained in Chapter 5)

  – identifying aspects of programmes of study and attainment targets that may present specific difficulties for individuals. In music, this might involve:

  – encouraging pupils who are hearing impaired to explore the effects of sound and perceive it in any way which they find accessible

  – giving time for visually impaired pupils to use one hand to read braille music whilst the other plays and vice versa, or giving them easy access to a tape that they can explore further whilst others have written notation

  – allowing a pupils with difficulty with motor skills to have more time to play and to use software with a step time facility to record their work

- developing pupils' self-esteem

- providing intellectual stimulation and to promote skills of more general application

Summary

Teachers are ultimately responsible for all the pupils they teach. In terms of participation, achievement, enjoyment – the buck stops here!

Pupils with a wide range of needs – physical/sensory, emotional, cognitive and social – are present in increasing numbers, in all mainstream settings.

Government policies point the way, with inclusion at the forefront of national policy – but it is up to teachers to make the rhetoric a reality.

Chapter 2 considers the music department's policy for special educational needs provision and inclusion, and how its development can shape classroom practice.

Departmental Policy

It is crucial that the music departmental policy describes a strategy for meeting pupils' special educational needs within this particular curricular area. The policy should set the scene for any visitor to the music department – from supply staff to inspectors, and parents/carers, and make an invaluable contribution to the departmental handbook. The process of developing a department SEN policy offers the opportunity to clarify and evaluate current thinking and practice within the music team (including peripatetic teachers and support staff) in order to establish a consistent approach.

In respect of including pupils with special educational needs the policy should:

- make the case for music – that it is a 'unique form of communication'

- clarify the responsibilities of all staff including peripatetic teachers and support staff and identify any with specialist training and/or knowledge

- describe the curriculum on offer and how it can be differentiated

- outline arrangements for assessment and reporting

- guide staff on how to work effectively with support staff

- identify staff training.

The starting point will be the school's SEN policy as required by the Education Act 1996, with each subject department 'fleshing out' the detail in a way which describes how things work in practice. The writing of a policy should be much more than a paper exercise completed to satisfy the senior management team and Ofsted inspectors: it is an opportunity for staff to come together as a team and create a framework for teaching music in a way that makes it accessible to all pupils in the school.

As music is likely to be a vital part of the lives of many pupils with SEN, getting the policy right is essential, and needs to be recognised by the senior staff in the school.

Where to start when writing a policy?

An audit can act as a starting point for reviewing current policy on SEN or to inform the writing of a new policy. It will involve gathering information and reviewing current practice with regard to pupils with SEN and is best completed by the whole of the department (both of you!), preferably with some additional advice from the SEN Co-ordinator or another member of staff with responsibility for SEN within the school. An audit carried out by the whole department can provide a valuable opportunity for professional development if it is seen as an exercise in sharing good practice and encouraging joint planning. For small departments such as music, this may best be done in joint sessions with music teachers from other local schools (your local Music Service may be able to help with this), but before embarking on an audit it is worth investing some time in a department meeting or training day, to raise awareness of special educational needs legislation and establish a shared philosophy. Appendix 2 contains an activity to use with staff. (These are also on the accompanying CD, with additional exercises you may choose to use.)

Useful headings when establishing a working policy

General Statement

- What does legislation and DfES guidance say?

- What does the school policy state?

- What do members of the department have to do to comply with it?

Definition of SEN

- What does SEN mean?

- What are the areas of need and the categories used in the Code of Practice?

- Are there any special implications within the subject area?

Provision for staff within the department

- How is information shared?

- Who has responsibility for SEN within the department?

- How and when is information shared?

- Where and what information is stored?

Provision for pupils with SEN

- How are pupils with SEN assessed and monitored in the department?
- How are contributions to IEPs and reviews made?
- What criteria are used for organising teaching groups?
- What alternative courses are offered to pupils with SEN?
- What special internal and external examination arrangements are made?
- What guidance is available for working with support staff?

Resources and learning materials

- Is there any specialist equipment used in the department?
- How are resources developed?
- Where are resources stored?

Staff qualifications and continuing professional development needs

- What qualifications do the members of the department have?
- What training has taken place?
- How is training planned?
- Is a record kept of training completed and training needs?

Monitoring and reviewing the policy

- How will the policy be monitored?
- When will the policy be reviewed?

The content of an SEN departmental policy

This section gives detailed information on what an SEN policy might include. Each heading is expanded with some detailed information and raises the main issues with regard to teaching pupils with SEN. The example statements can be personalised and brought together to make a policy. An example policy is included on the accompanying CD and in Appendix 3.

General statement with reference to the school's SEN policy

All schools must have an SEN policy according to the Education Act 1996. This policy will set out basic information on the school's SEN provision, how the school identifies, assesses and provides for pupils with SEN, including information on staffing and working in partnership with other professionals and parents.

Any department policy needs to have reference to the school SEN policy, and should state that all members of the department will ensure that the needs of all pupils with SEN are met, according to the aims of the school and its SEN policy.

Definition of SEN

It is useful to insert at least the four areas of SEN in the department policy, as used in the Code of Practice for Special Educational Needs.

TABLE 2.1 THE FOUR AREAS OF SEN

Cognition and Learning Needs	Behaviour, Emotional and Social Development Needs	Communication and Interaction Needs	Sensory and/or Physical Needs
Specific learning difficulties (SpLD) Dyslexia Moderate learning difficulties (MLD) Severe learning difficulties (SLD) Profound and multiple learning difficulties (PMLD)	Behaviour, emotional and social difficulties (BESD) Attention Deficit Disorder (ADD) Attention Deficit Hyperactivity Disorder (ADHD)	Speech, language and communication needs Autistic Spectrum Disorder (ASD) Asperger's Syndrome	Hearing impairment (HI) Visual impairment (VI) Multi-sensory impairment (MSI) Physical difficulties (PD)

Provision for staff within the department

Music, like art and drama, tends to be a small department and one person may be teaching all pupils in the school, if only once a week. It is, in our opinion, a good idea to have a 'second–in-charge' even if they only teach a few lessons of music. This gives someone to bounce ideas off and also someone else to share the flak should other subject teachers refuse to let pupils out for peripatetic lessons.

In other departments a member of staff is nominated to have special responsibility for SEN provision, (with or without remuneration). This is likely to be the Head of Department in Music because of the implications for capitation in regard of differentiated instruments and equipment.

The responsibilities of this post may include liaison with the SENCO, attending any liaison meetings and providing feedback via meetings and minutes, attending training, maintaining the departmental SEN information and records and representing the need of pupils with SEN at departmental level. This post can be seen as a valuable development opportunity for staff. The name of this person should be included in the policy.

It is usual for the music department to be part of the Expressive/Creative Arts Faculty. Although each pupil's individual Special Needs may be met quite differently within these different areas, Art, Drama, Dance, Photography etc. will share a common philosophy and it may therefore be helpful to have an Expressive Arts SEN representative.

Setting out how members of the department raise concerns about pupils with SEN can be included in this section. Concerns may be raised at specified departmental meetings before referral to the SENCO. An identified member of the department could make referrals to the SENCO and keep a record of this information.

Here it may be appropriate to detail any outside peripatetic support staff and music therapists in the area.

Reference to working with teaching assistants and other support staff will include a commitment to planning and communication between staff. There may be information on inviting support staff to meetings, resources and lesson plans.

A reference to the centrally held lists of pupils with SEN and other relevant information will also be included in this section. A note about confidentiality of information should be included. It cannot be stressed too often that confidentiality is vital to the self-esteem and general well-being of the pupil with SEN. Details of their toilet habits or their dysfunctional home life or periods of abuse should be known to as few members of staff as is strictly necessary. It may however be relevant to know if certain pupils have suffered some abuse in the past, and so that on no account should they be touched or approached suddenly from behind.

Provision for pupils with SEN

It is the responsibility of all staff to know which pupils have SEN and to identify any pupils having difficulties. Music teachers are going to hear about pupils with SEN from other subject teachers and agencies (support staff, SENCO etc.) because in a lesson held only once a week picking up who has Special Needs is not always easy. Ways in which pupils with SEN can be identified would come from the following:

- observation in lessons

- assessment of class work

- homework tasks

- end of module tests

- progress checks

- primary school reports

- parents' comments

- annual examinations

- reports

Setting out how pupils with SEN are grouped within the music department may include specifying the criteria used and/or the philosophy behind the method of grouping. This has implications for cross-departmental settings. It is very important that music is set according to arts department criteria and not according to the needs of any other department (i.e. it should not be a time tabling compromise). Alas, how often is music set with RE and PE or even MFL?

All music groups involve pupils of differing abilities musically, and a pupil's ability in music may be inversely proportional to their other abilities. It is certainly not going to be necessarily closely related. It can sometimes take music teachers by surprise when they read the written work of pupils they have previously only ever seen as fluent music players. So, setting by ability is not usually relevant to music, and the policy statement may reflect this.

'The pupils are taught in their tutor groups as Music and the Arts provide particular opportunities for pupils in their social development.'

There should be no reason, and there is certainly little opportunity, for pupils to move between groups. A tutor group is a place where a pupil first finds her/his identity. Working in whole class musical ensembles and listening to each other's performances is when music can reinforce this feeling of identity and also security.

Special Examination arrangements need to be considered not only at Key Stages 3 and 4 but also for internal examinations. How and when these will be discussed should be clarified. Reference to SENCO and examination arrangements from the examination board should be taken into account. Recognition that staff in the department understand the current legislation and guidance from central government is important so a reference to the SEN Code of Practice and the levels of SEN intervention is helpful within the policy. Here is a good place also to put a statement about the school behaviour policy and rewards and sanctions, and how the department will make any necessary adjustments to meet the needs of pupils with SEN.

Here too is the place to remember that Special Needs may not be the barrier in music that it is in other subjects. This may be a good place to argue that pupils who need to be withdrawn for extra language work, or speech therapy or circle time etc., should not be taken out of their once-a-week music lesson, as the difficulties that may pertain in maths may not be true in music.

Here it should be stated that it is understood that pupils with SEN may receive additional support if they have a statement of SEN, or are at School Action Plus or School Action. The staff in the music department will aim to support the pupils to achieve their targets as specified on their IEPs and will provide feedback for IEP or Statement reviews. Pupils with SEN will be included in the departmental monitoring system used for all pupils. Additional support will be requested as appropriate.

Pupils with behaviour problems will also have detailed Individual Behaviour Plans which detail potential problems and the series of responses as devised by the SENCO or the Learning Base/Behaviour Support Department (in possible consultation with the Head of Music) (see CD for exemplars).

Resources and learning materials

The department policy needs to specify what differentiated materials are available, where they are kept and how to find new resources. This section could include a statement about working with support staff to develop resources or access specialist resources as needed and the use of ICT. Teaching strategies may also be identified if appropriate. Advice on more specialist equipment can be sought as necessary, possibly through LEA support services: contact details may be available from the SENCO, or the department may have direct links .

Any specially bought subject text or alternative/appropriate courses can be specified as well as any external assessment and examination courses.

Example

> The department will provide suitably differentiated materials and, where appropriate, specialist resources for pupils with SEN. Instruments and equipment will be tailored to each pupil's needs (these are identified in Chapter 5).

Staff qualifications and Continuing Professional Development needs

It is important to recognise and record the qualifications and special skills gained by staff within the department. Training can include not only external courses but also in-house INSET and opportunities such as observing other staff, working to produce materials with other staff, and visiting other establishments. Staff may have hidden skills that might enhance the work of the department and the school: for example, some staff might be proficient in the use of sign language.

Example

> A record of training undertaken, specialist skills and training required will be kept in the department handbook. Requests for training will be considered in line with the department and school improvement plan.

Monitoring and reviewing the policy

To be effective any policy needs regular monitoring and review. These can be planned as part of the yearly cycle. The responsibility for the monitoring can rest with the Head of Department but will have more effect if supported by someone from outside acting as a critical friend. This could be the SENCO or a member of the senior management team in school.

Example

> The Department SEN policy will be monitored by the Head of Faculty on a planned annual basis, with advice being sought from the SENCO as part of a three-yearly review process.

Summary

Creating a departmental SEN policy should be a developmental activity to improve the teaching and learning for all pupils but especially those with special or additional needs. The policy should be a working document that will evolve and change; it is there to challenge current practice and to encourage improvement for both pupils and staff. If departmental staff work together to create the policy, they will have ownership of it; it will have true meaning and be effective in clarifying practice.

Many pupils with SEN may have a unique contribution to a music lesson. Music may be the one activity they can do extremely well and this needs to be discovered and encouraged.

CHAPTER 3

Different Types of SEN

This chapter is a starting point for information on the special educational needs most frequently occurring in the mainstream secondary school. It describes the main characteristics of each learning difficulty with practical ideas for use in music lessons, and contacts for further information. Some of the tips are based on good secondary practice whilst others encourage teachers to try new or less familiar approaches.

The special educational needs in this chapter are grouped under the headings used in the SEN Revised Code of Practice (DfES 2001):

- cognition and learning

- behaviour, emotional and social development

- communication and interaction

- sensory and/or physical needs.
  (See Table 2.1 in Chapter 2.)

The labels used in this chapter are useful when describing pupils' difficulties but it is important to remember not to use the label in order to define the pupil. Put the pupil before the difficulty, saying 'the pupil with special educational needs' rather than 'the SEN pupil', 'Pupils with MLD' rather than 'MLDs'.

Remember to take care in using labels when talking with parents, pupils or other professionals. Unless a pupil has a firm diagnosis, and parents and pupil understand the implications of that diagnosis, it is more appropriate to describe the features of the special educational need rather than use the label. For example a teacher might describe a pupil's spelling difficulties but not use the term 'dyslexic'.

The number and profile of pupils with special educational needs will vary from school to school, so it is important to consider the pupil with SEN as an individual within your school and subject environment. The strategies contained in this chapter will help teachers adapt that environment to meet the needs of individual pupils within the subject context. For example, rather than saying,

'He can't read the worksheet', recognise that the worksheet is too difficult for the pupil, and adapt the work accordingly.

There is a continuum of need within each of the special educational needs listed here. Some pupils will be affected more than others, and show fewer or more of the characteristics described.

The availability and levels of support from professionals within a school (e.g. SENCOs, support teachers, teaching assistants) and external professionals (e.g. educational psychologists, Learning Support Service staff, medical staff) will depend on the severity of pupils' SEN. This continuum of need will also impact on the subject teacher's planning and allocation of support staff.

Pupils with other less common special educational needs may be included in some secondary schools, and additional information on these conditions may be found in a variety of sources. These include the school SENCO, LEA support services, educational psychologists and the internet.

Asperger's Syndrome

Asperger's Syndrome is a disorder at the able end of the autistic spectrum. People with Asperger's Syndrome have average to high intelligence but share the same Triad of Impairments. They often want to make friends but do not understand the complex rules of social interaction. They have impaired fine and gross motor skills with writing being a particular problem. Boys are more likely to be affected – with the ratio being 10:1 boys to girls. Because they appear 'odd' and naïve, these pupils are particularly vulnerable to bullying.

Main characteristics

- **Social interaction**
  Pupils with Asperger's Syndrome want friends but have not developed the strategies necessary for making and sustaining friendships. They find it very difficult to learn social norms and to pick up on social cues. High social situations, such as lessons, can cause great anxiety.
- **Social communication**
  Pupils have appropriate spoken language but tend to sound formal and pedantic, using little expression and with an unusual tone of voice. They have difficulty using and understanding non-verbal language such as facial expression, gesture, body language and eye-contact. They have a literal understanding of language and do not grasp implied meanings.
- **Social imagination**
  Pupils with Asperger's Syndrome need structured environments, and to have routines they understand and can anticipate. They excel at learning facts and figures, but have difficulty understanding abstract concepts and in generalising information and skills. They often have all-consuming special interests.

How can the music teacher help?

- Maintain the same routine in lessons.
- Liaise closely with parents, especially over homework.
- Create as calm a classroom environment as possible.
- Provide separate listening facilities if possible.
- Allow the pupil to sit in the same place for each lesson.
- Set up a work buddy system for your lessons.
- Provide additional visual cues in class, including visual timetables and task activity lists.
- Give time to process questions and respond.
- Make sure pupils understand what to do.
- Allow alternatives to writing for recording.
- Be aware that the pupil may be over-sensitive to out of tune instruments and singing. Prepare for changes to routines well in advance.
- Give written homework instructions and stick into an exercise book.
- Have your own class rules and apply them consistently.
- Provide opportunities for more able musicians to perform for others.

The National Autistic Society, 393 City Road, London EC1V 1NG
Tel: 0870 600 8585 Helpline (10am–4pm, Mon–Fri)
Tel: 020 7833 2299 Fax: 020 7833 9666
Email: nas@nas.org.uk Website: http://www.nas.org.uk

Attention Deficit Disorder (with or without hyperactivity) ADD/ADHD

Attention Deficit Hyperactivity Disorder is a term used to describe children who are overactive or exceptionally impulsive, and who have difficulty in paying attention. It is caused by a form of brain dysfunction of a genetic nature. ADHD can sometimes be controlled effectively by medication. Children of all levels of ability can have ADHD.

Main characteristics

- difficulty in following instructions and completing tasks
- easily distracted by noise, movement of others, objects attracting attention
- often doesn't listen when spoken to
- fidgets and becomes restless, can't sit still
- interferes with other pupil's work
- can't stop talking, interrupts others, calls out
- runs about when inappropriate
- has difficulty in waiting or taking turns
- acts impulsively without thinking about the consequences (e.g. starts playing an instrument before understanding what is required)

How can the music teacher help?

- Make eye contact and use the pupil's name when speaking to him.
- Keep instructions simple – the one sentence rule.
- Provide clear routines and rules and rehearse them regularly.
- Sit the pupil away from obvious distractions e.g. windows, the computer.
- In busy situations direct the pupil by name to visual or practical objects.
- Encourage the pupil to repeat back instructions before starting work.
- Tell the pupil when to start a task.
- Give two choices – avoid the option of the pupil saying 'No' by asking 'Do you want to play keyboard or drums?
- Give advanced warning when something is about to happen. Change or finish with a time, e.g. 'in two minutes I need you (pupil name) to . . . '.
- Give specific praise – catch him being good, give attention for positive behaviour.
- Give the pupil responsibilities so that others can see him in a positive light and he develops a positive self image.
- Use a lot of ensemble work, call and response; let them count songs in.

ADD Information Services, PO Box 340, Edgware, Middlesex HA8 9HL
Tel: 020 8906 9068
ADDNET UK website: www.btinternet.com/~black.ice/addnet/

Autistic Spectrum Disorders (ASD)

The term 'Autistic Spectrum Disorders' is used for a range of disorders affecting the development of social interaction, social communication and social imagination and flexibility of thought. This is known as the 'Triad of Impairments'. Pupils with ASD cover the full range of ability, and the severity of the impairment varies widely. Some pupils also have learning disabilities or other difficulties. Four times as many boys as girls are diagnosed with an ASD.

Main characteristics

- **Social interaction**
  Pupils with an ASD find it difficult to understand social behaviour and this affects their ability to interact with children and adults. They do not always understand social contexts. They may experience high levels of stress and anxiety in settings that do not meet their needs or when routines are changed. This can lead to inappropriate behaviour.

- **Social communication**
  Understanding and use of non-verbal and verbal communication is impaired. Pupils with an ASD have difficulty understanding the communication of others and in developing effective communication themselves. They have a literal understanding of language. Many are delayed in learning to speak, and some never develop speech at all.

- **Social imagination and flexibility of thought**
  Pupils with an ASD have difficulty in thinking and behaving flexibly which may result in restricted, obsessional, or repetitive activities. They are often more interested in objects than people, and may have intense interests in one particular area, such as trains and vacuum cleaners. Pupils work best when they have a routine. Unexpected changes in those routines will cause distress. Some pupils with autistic spectrum disorders have a different perception of sounds, sights, smell, touch, and taste, and this can affect their response to these sensations.

How can the music teacher help?

- Liaise with parents as they will have many useful strategies.

- Provide visual supports in class; objects, pictures etc.

- Give a symbolic or written timetable for each day.

- Give advance warning of any changes to usual routines.

- Provide either an individual desk or with a work buddy.

- Avoid using too much eye contact as it can cause distress.

- Give individual instructions using the pupil's name, e.g. 'Paul, bring me your book'.

- Allow access to computers.

- Develop social interactions using a buddy system or Circle of Friends.

- Avoid using metaphor, idiom or sarcasm – say what you mean in simple language.

- Use special interests to motivate.

- Allow difficult situations to be rehearsed by means of Social Stories.

- Accept and affirm their way of doing things.

- Allow pupils with an ASD to work solo some of the time, giving opportunities for them to explore all the intricacies of an instrument and approach the music in their own particular timescale.

BEHAVIOURAL, EMOTIONAL AND SOCIAL DEVELOPMENT NEEDS

This term includes behavioural, emotional, social difficulties and Attention Deficit Disorder with or without hyperactivity. These difficulties can be seen across the whole ability range and have a continuum of severity. Pupils with special educational needs in this category are those that have persistent difficulties despite an effective school behaviour policy and a personal and social curriculum.

Behavioural, emotional, social difficulties (BESD)

Main characteristics

- inattentive, poor concentration and lacks interest in school/school work
- easily frustrated, anxious about changes
- unable to work in groups
- unable to work independently, constantly seeking help
- confrontational – verbally aggressive towards pupils and/or adults
- physically aggressive towards pupils and/or adults
- destroys property – their own/others
- appears withdrawn, distressed, unhappy, sulky, may self harm
- lacks confidence, acts extremely frightened, lacks self-esteem
- finds it difficult to communicate
- finds it difficult to accept praise

How can the music teacher help?

- Check the ability level of the pupil and adapt the level of work to this. Some pupils with BESD will pick up music skills very quickly.
- Consider the pupil's strengths and use them.
- Tell the pupil what you expect in advance, as regards work and behaviour.
- Talk to the pupil to find out a bit about them.
- Set a subject target with a reward system.
- Focus your comments on the behaviour not on the pupil, and offer an alternative way of behaving when correcting the pupil.
- Use positive language and verbal praise whenever possible.
- Tell the pupil what you want them to do: 'I need you to . . .', rather than ask. This avoids confrontation and allows room for negotiation.
- Give the pupil a choice between two options.
- Stick to what you say.
- Involve the pupil in responsibilities to increase self-esteem and confidence.
- Almost casually, give out small snippets of honest praise.
- Plan a 'time out' system. Ask a colleague for help with this.
- Have more than one of each instrument, if possible all the same. Buy top-quality robust instruments, such as Coomber tape recording machines.

SEBDA: the Association of Workers for Children with Emotional and Behavioural Difficulties.
Website: http://www.awcebd.co.uk

Cerebral palsy (CP)

Cerebral palsy is a persistent disorder of movement and posture. It is caused by damage or lack of development to part of the brain before or during birth or in early childhood. Problems vary from slight clumsiness to more severe lack of control of movements. Pupils with CP may also have learning difficulties. They may use a wheelchair or other mobility aid.

Main characteristics

There are three main forms of Cerebral palsy:

- *spasticity* – disordered control of movement associated with stiffened muscles

- *athetosis* – frequent involuntary movements

- *ataxia* – an unsteady gait with balance difficulties and poor spatial awareness

  Pupils may also have communication difficulties.

How can the music teacher help?

- Talk to parents, the physiotherapist – and the pupil.

- Consider the classroom layout.

- Have high academic expectations.

- Use visual supports; objects, pictures, symbols.

- Arrange a work/subject buddy.

- Speak directly to the pupil rather than through a teaching assistant and be aware that pupils may understand speech even when they have limited expressive communication.

- Ensure access to appropriate IT equipment for the subject – and that it is used.

- Investigate adapted instruments and music technology equipment such as wrist bells, rainsticks, Boomwhackers (available from Rompa at www.rompa.com) and Soundbeam (www.soundbeam.co.uk).

Scope, PO BOX 833, Milton Keynes MK12 5NY
Tel: 0808 800 3333 (Freephone helpline) Fax: 01908 321051
Email: cphelpline@scope.org.uk Website: http://www.scope.org.uk

Down's Syndrome (DS)

Down's Syndrome is the most common identifiable cause of learning disability. This is a genetic condition caused by the presence of an extra chromosome 21. People with DS have varying degrees of learning difficulties ranging from mild to severe. They have a specific learning profile with characteristic strengths and weaknesses. All share certain physical characteristics but will also inherit family traits, in physical features and personality. They may have additional sight, hearing, respiratory and heart problems.

Main characteristics

- delayed motor skills

- take longer to learn and consolidate new skills

- limited concentration

- difficulties with generalisation, thinking and reasoning

- sequencing difficulties

- stronger visual than aural skills

- better social than academic skills

- likely to adore music and be uninhibited in performance

- likely to be obstinate

How can the music teacher help?

- Sit where best able to see and hear.

- Speak directly to pupil and reinforce with facial expression, pictures and objects. Use simple, familiar language in short sentences.

- Check instructions have been understood.

- Give time to process information and formulate a response.

- Break lessons up into a series of shorter, varied, and achievable tasks.

- Set differentiated tasks linked to the work of the rest of the class.

- Allow working in top sets to give good behaviour models.

- Provide a work buddy, but expect unsupported work for part of each lesson.

The Down's Syndrome Association, 155 Mitcham Road, London SW17 9PG
Tel: 020 8682 4001 Email: info@downs-syndrome.org.uk
Website: http://www.downs-syndrome.org.uk

Fragile X Syndrome

Fragile X Syndrome is caused by a malformation of the X chromosome and is the most common form of inherited learning disability. This intellectual disability varies widely, with up to a third having learning problems ranging from moderate to severe. More boys than girls are affected but both may be carriers.

Main characteristics

- delayed and disordered speech and language development
- difficulties with the social use of language
- articulation and/or fluency difficulties
- verbal skills better developed than reasoning skills
- repetitive or obsessive behaviour such as hand-flapping, chewing etc.
- clumsiness and fine motor co-ordination problems
- attention deficit and hyperactivity
- easily anxious or overwhelmed in busy environments

How can the music teacher help?

- Liaise with parents.
- Make sure pupil knows what is to happen in each lesson – visual timetables, work schedules or written lists.
- Sit at front of class, in the same seat for all lessons.
- Arrange a work/subject buddy.
- Where possible keep to routines and give prior warning of all changes.
- Make instructions clear and simple.
- Use lots of repetition.
- Use visual supports; objects, pictures, symbols.
- Allow to use computer to record and access information.
- Give lots of praise and positive feedback.

Fragile X Society, Rood End House, 6 Stortford Road, Dunmow CM6 1DA
Tel: 01434 813147 (Helpline) Tel: 01371 875100 (Office)
Email: info@fragilex.org.uk Website: http://www.fragilex.org.uk

Moderate learning difficulties (MLD)

The term moderate learning difficulties is used to describe pupils who find it extremely difficult to achieve expected levels of attainment across the curriculum even with a differentiated and flexible approach. These pupils do not find learning easy and can suffer from low self-esteem and sometime exhibit unacceptable behaviour as a way of avoiding failure.

Main characteristics

- difficulties with reading, writing and comprehension
- immature social and emotional skills
- limited vocabulary and communication skills
- short attention span
- under developed co-ordination skills
- lack of logical reasoning
- inability to transfer and apply skills to different situations
- have difficulty remembering what has been taught
- difficulty with organising themselves, following a timetable, remembering books and equipment

How can the music teacher help?

- Check the pupil's strengths, weaknesses and attainment levels.
- Establish a routine within the lesson.
- Keep tasks short, varied and achievable.
- Keep listening tasks short or broken up with activities.
- Provide word lists, writing frames, shorten text.
- Check previously gained knowledge and build on this.
- Repeat information in different ways. Check understanding.
- Show the child what to do or what the expected outcome is.
- Use lots of praise, instant rewards – catch them trying hard.
- Be firm.

The MLD Alliance, c/o The Elfrida Society, 34 Islington Park Street, London N1 1PX
www.mldalliance.com/executive.htm

Physical disability (PD)

There is a wide range of physical disabilities, and pupils with PD cover all academic abilities. Some pupils are able to access the curriculum and learn effectively without additional educational provision. They have a disability but do not have a special educational need. For other pupils the impact on their education may be severe, and the school will need to make adjustments to enable them to access the curriculum.

Some pupils with a physical disability have associated medical conditions which may impact on their mobility. These include cerebral palsy, heart disease, spina bifida and hydrocephalus, and muscular dystrophy. Pupils with physical disabilities may also have sensory impairments, neurological problems, or learning difficulties. They may use a wheelchair and/or additional mobility aids. Some pupils will be mobile but may have significant fine motor difficulties which require support. Others may need augmentative or alternative communication aids.

Pupils with a physical disability may need to miss lessons to attend physiotherapy or medical appointments. They are also likely to become very tired as they expend greater effort to complete everyday tasks. Schools will need to be flexible and sensitive to individual pupil needs.

How can the music teacher help?

- Get to know pupils and parents and they will help you make the right adjustments.

- Maintain high expectations.

- Consider the classroom layout.

- Allow to leave lessons a few minutes early to avoid busy corridors and give time to get to the next lesson.

- Give them priority getting into music practice rooms.

- Set homework earlier in the lesson so instructions are not missed.

- Speak directly to the pupil rather than through a teaching assistant, and wait for them to reply.

- Let pupils make their own decisions.

- Ensure access to appropriate IT equipment for the lesson – and that it is used!

- Give alternative ways of recording work.

- Plan to cover work missed through medical or physiotherapy appointments.

- Be sensitive to fatigue, especially at the end of the school day.

- Allow for musical 'scribble'.

Semantic Pragmatic Disorder (SPD)

Semantic Pragmatic Disorder is a communication disorder which falls within the autistic spectrum. Semantic refers to the meanings of words and phrases and pragmatic refers to the use of language in a social context. Pupils with this disorder have difficulties understanding the meaning of what people say and in using language to communicate effectively.

Pupils with SPD find it difficult to extract the central meaning – saliency – of situations.

Main characteristics

- delayed language development
- fluent speech but may sound stilted or over-formal
- may repeat phrases out of context from videos or adult conversations
- difficulty understanding abstract concepts
- limited or inappropriate use of eye contact, facial expression or gesture
- motor skills problems

How can the music teacher help?

- Sit at front of the room to avoid distractions.
- Use visual supports; objects, pictures, symbols.
- Pair with a work/subject buddy.
- Create a calm working environment with clear classroom rules.
- Be specific and unambiguous when giving instructions.
- Make sure instructions are understood, especially when using subject specific vocabulary that can have another meaning in a different context.

AFASIC, 2nd Floor, 50–52 Great Sutton Street, London EC1V 0DJ
Tel: 0845 355 5577 (Helpline 11a.m. to 2p.m.)
Tel: 020 7490 9410 Fax: 020 7251 2834
Email: info@afasic.org.uk Website: http://www.afasic.org.uk

Sensory impairments

Hearing impairment (HI)

The term hearing impairment is a generic term used to describe all hearing loss. The main types of loss are monaural, conductive, sensory and mixed loss. The degree of hearing loss is described as mild, moderate, severe or profound. Deaf children and their parents/carers generally prefer the term 'deaf' to describe their condition.

Hearing loss, particularly when mild, and/or temporary, is often a hidden disability.

How can the music teacher help?

- Ask about the degree of hearing loss the pupil has.

- Check the best seating position (e.g. away from the hum of OHP or computers, with good ear to speaker).

- Check that the pupil can see your face for facial expressions and lip reading.

- Provide a list of vocabulary, context and visual clues especially for new subjects.

- During class discussion allow one pupil to speak at a time and indicate where the speaker is.

- Check that any aids are working and if there is any other specialist equipment available.

- Increase the visual input.

- Have a signer, and check the position of the signer.

- Allow pupils to experiment on a range of musical instruments.

Royal Institute for the Deaf (RNID), 19–23 Featherstone St, London EC1Y 8SL
Tel: 0808 808 0123
British Deaf Association (BDA), 1–3 Worship St, London EC2A 2AB
British Association of Teachers of the Deaf (BATOD), The Orchard, Leven, North Humberside, HU17 5QA
www.batod.org.uk

Visual impairment (VI)

Visual impairment refers to a range of difficulties, including those experienced by pupils with monocular vision (vision in one eye), those who are partially sighted and those who are blind. Pupils with visual impairment cover the whole ability range and some pupils may have other SEN.

How can the music teacher help?

- Check the optimum position for the pupil e.g. for a monocular pupil their good eye should be towards the action.

- Check that glasses are worn if they have been prescribed.

- If the pupil wears glasses, check that they are clean.

- Always provide the pupil with his own (enlarged) copy of the text/music.

- Make full use of ICT.

- Do not stand with your back to the window as this creates a silhouette and makes it harder for the pupil to see you.

- Draw the pupil's attention to displays – which they may not notice.

- Make sure the floor is kept free of clutter.

- Tell the pupil if there is a change to the layout of a space.

- Warn pupils about any sudden sounds.

- Work out a system of providing non-visual cues when playing instruments.

Royal National Institute for the Blind (RNIB) 105 Judd Street, London WC1H 9NE
Tel: 020 7388 1266
Fax: 020 7388 2034
www.rnid.org.uk

Multi-sensory impairment

Pupils with multi-sensory impairment have a combination of visual and hearing difficulties. They may also have other additional disabilities that make their situation complex. A pupil with these difficulties is likely to have a high level of individual support.

Music is an important subject for pupils with multi-sensory impairments. Pupils will experience music in different ways, through hearing, feeling vibrations or a combination of both. Music teachers can help pupils to make sense of the sounds they hear by giving them opportunities to experiment with sounds and to work alongside other students in pairs and ensembles.

How can the music teacher help?

- The subject teacher will need to liaise with support staff to ascertain the appropriate provision within each subject.

- Consideration will need to be given to alternative means of communication.

- Be prepared to be flexible and to adapt tasks, targets and assessment procedures.

- Allow pupils to create and control sounds, helping them to make the link between the source of the sound and the sound itself e.g. hitting a cymbal and feeling the resulting vibrations with their hands.

Severe learning difficulties (SLD)

This term covers a wide and varied group of pupils who have significant intellectual or cognitive impairments. Many have communication difficulties and/or sensory impairments in addition to more general cognitive impairments. They may also have difficulties in mobility, co-ordination and perception. Some pupils may use signs and symbols to support their communication and understanding. Their attainments may be within or below level 1 of the National Curriculum, or in the upper P scale range (P4–P8), for much of their school careers.

How can the music teacher help?

- Liaise with parents.

- Arrange a work/subject buddy.

- Use visual supports; objects, pictures, symbols.

- Learn some signs relevant to the subject.

- Allow time to process information and formulate responses.

- Set differentiated tasks linked to the work of the rest of the class.

- Set achievable targets for each lesson or module of work.

- Accept different recording methods; drawings, audio or video recordings, photographs etc.

- Give access to computers where appropriate.

- Use a multi-sensory approach.

- Give a series of short, varied activities within each lesson.

Profound and multiple learning difficulties (PMLD)

Pupils with profound and multiple learning difficulties have complex learning needs. In addition to very severe learning difficulties, pupils have other significant difficulties, such as physical disabilities, sensory impairments or severe medical conditions. Pupils with PMLD require a high level of adult support, both for their learning needs and for their personal care.

They are able to access the curriculum through sensory experiences and stimulation. Some pupils communicate by gesture, eye pointing or symbols, others by very simple language. Their attainments are likely to remain in the early P scale range (P1–P4) throughout their school careers (that is below level 1 of the National Curriculum). The P scales provide small, achievable steps to monitor progress. Some pupils will make no progress or may even regress because of associated medical conditions. For this group, experiences are as important as attainment.

How can the music teacher help?

- Liaise with parents and teaching assistants.

- Consider the classroom layout.

- Identify possible sensory experiences in your lessons.

- Use additional sensory supports; objects, pictures, fragrances, music, movements, food etc.

- Take photographs to record experiences and responses.

- Set up a work/subject buddy rota for the class.

- Identify times when the pupil can work with groups.

- Interact with pupils as much as possible and encourage interaction between pupils. Encourage the pupil to participate – but don't force them.

MENCAP, 117–123 Golden Lane,
London EC1Y 0RT
Tel: 020 7454 0454 Website: http://www.mencap.org.uk

SPECIFIC LEARNING DIFFICULTIES (SPLD)

The term Specific Learning Difficulties covers Dyslexia, Dyscalculia and Dyspraxia.

Dyslexia

The term 'dyslexia' is used to describe a learning difficulty associated with words and it can affect a pupil's ability to read, write and/or spell. Research has shown that there is no one definitive definition of dyslexia or one identified cause, and it has a wide range of symptoms. Although found across a whole range of ability levels, the idea that dyslexia presents as a difficulty between expected outcomes and performance is widely held. Music is likely to be a powerful release for pupils struggling with the frustrations associated with underachievement.

Main characteristics

- Pupils may frequently lose their place, make a lot of errors with the high frequency words, have difficulty reading names and have difficult blending sounds and segmenting words. Reading requires a great deal of effort and concentration.

- Pupils' work may seem messy with crossing outs, similarly shaped letters may be confused, such as b/d/p/q, m/w, n/u, and letters in words may be jumbled: tired/tried. Spelling difficulties often persist into adult life and these pupils become reluctant writers.

- Western notation may cause problems.

How can the music teacher help?

- Be aware of the type of difficulty and the pupil's strengths.

- Teach and allow the use of word processing, spell checkers and computer aided learning packages.

- Provide word lists and photocopies of copying from the board.

- Consider alternative recording methods e.g. pictures, plans, flow charts, mind maps.

- Allow extra time for tasks including assessments and examinations.

- Focus on aural work, and investigate different systems of notation.

The British Dyslexia Association
Tel: 0118 966 8271 www.bda-dyslexia.org.uk
Dyslexia Institute
Tel: 07184 463 851 www.dyslexia-inst.org.uk

Dyscalculia

The term 'dyscalculia' is used to describe a difficulty in mathematics. This might be either a marked discrepancy between the pupil's developmental level and general ability on measures of specific maths ability or a total inability to abstract or consider concepts and numbers.

Main characteristics

- The pupil may have difficulty counting by rote, writing or reading numbers, miss out or reverse numbers, have difficulty with mental maths, and be unable to remember concepts, rules and formulae.

- Many have difficulty with money, telling the time, with directions, and with right and left, with sequencing events or losing track of turns e.g. in team games, dance.

- Pupils may have a problem with notation.

How can the music teacher help?

- Provide number/word/rule/formulae lists and photocopies of copying from the board.

- Make use of ICT and teach the use of calculators.

- Encourage the use of rough paper for working out.

- Plan the setting out of work, with the work well spaced on the page.

- Provide practical objects that are age appropriate to aid learning.

- Allow extra time for tasks, including assessments and examinations.

- Explore different forms of notation [e.g. Foxwood songsheets], use big clear boxes and break the music down into manageable units.

www.dyscalculia.co.uk

Dyspraxia

The term 'dyspraxia' is used to describe an immaturity with the way in which the brain processes information, resulting in messages not being properly transmitted.

Main characteristics

- difficulty in co-ordinating movements, may appear awkward and clumsy

- difficulty with handwriting and drawing, throwing and catching

- difficulty following sequential events, e.g. multiple instructions

- may misinterpret situations, take things literally

- limited social skills and become frustrated and irritable

- some articulation difficulties (see verbal dyspraxia)

- may have good fine motor skills – need to check this out

How can the music teacher help?

- Be sensitive to the pupil's limitations in games and outdoor activities and plan tasks to enable success.

- Ask the pupil questions to check his/her understanding of instructions/tasks.

- Check seating position to encourage good presentation (both feet resting on the floor, desk at elbow height and, ideally, with a sloping surface to work on).

- Be patient and prepare to be surprised.

Website: www.dyspraxiafoundation.org.uk

Speech, language and communication difficulties (SLCD)

Pupils with SLCD have problems understanding what others say and/or making others understand what they say. Any problem affecting speech, language and communication will have a significant effect on a pupil's self-esteem, and personal and social relationships. The development of literacy skills is also likely to be affected. Even where pupils learn to decode, they may not understand what they have read. Sign language gives pupils an additional method of communication.

Pupils with speech, language and communication difficulties cover the whole range of academic abilities.

Music, however, is a form of communication which can bypass difficulties with speech and language, and can enable the child to communicate in another mode; singing, playing an instrument, conducting etc.

Main characteristics

- **Speech difficulties**
  Pupils who have difficulties with expressive language may experience problems in articulation and the production of speech sounds, or in co-ordinating the muscles that control speech. They may have a stammer or some other form of dysfluency.
- **Language/communication difficulties**
  Pupils with receptive language impairments have difficulty understanding the meaning of what others say. They may use words incorrectly with inappropriate grammatical patterns, have a reduced vocabulary, or find it hard to recall words and express ideas. Pupils may also have difficulty using and understanding eye-contact, facial expression, gesture and body language.

How can the music teacher help?

- Talk to parents, speech therapist – and the pupil.
- Learn the most common signs for your subject.
- Use visual supports; objects, pictures, symbols.
- Use the pupil's name when addressing them.
- Give one instruction at a time, using short, simple sentences.
- Give time to respond before repeating a question.
- Make sure pupils understand what they have to do before starting a task.
- Pair with a work/subject buddy.
- Give written homework instructions.

ICAN 4, Dyer's Buildings, Holborn, London EC1N 2QP Tel: 0870 010 4066
Email: info@ican.org.uk Website: http://www.ican.org.uk
AFASIC 2nd Floor, 50–52 Great Sutton Street, London EC1V 0DJ
Tel: 0845 355 5577 (Helpline) Tel: 020 7490 9410 Fax: 020 7251 2834
Email: info@afasic.org.uk Website: http://www.afasic.org.uk

Tourette's Syndrome (TS)

Tourette's Syndrome is a neurological disorder characterised by tics. Tics are involuntary rapid or sudden movements or sounds that are frequently repeated. There is a wide range of severity of the condition with some people having no need to seek medical help while others have a socially disabling condition. The tics can be suppressed for a short time but will be more noticeable when the pupil is anxious or excited.

Main characteristics

Physical tics

Range from simple blinking or nodding through more complex movements to more extreme conditions such as echopraxia (imitating actions seen) or copropraxia (repeatedly making obscene gestures).

Vocal tics

Vocal tics may be as simple as throat clearing or coughing but can progress to be as extreme as echolalia (the repetition of what was last heard) or coprolalia (the repetition of obscene words).

Tourette's Syndrome itself causes no behavioural or educational problems but other, associated disorders such as Attention Deficit Hyperactivity Disorder (ADHD) or Obsessive Compulsive Disorder (OCD) may be present.

Music can affect children with Tourette's Syndrome in different ways. It may have a calming influence or it can make the pupil excited and so make the vocal and physical tics worse.

How can the music teacher help?

- Establish a rapport with the pupil.

- Talk to the parents.

- Agree an 'escape route' signal should the tics become disruptive.

- Allow the pupil to sit at the back of the room to prevent staring.

- Give access to a computer to reduce handwriting.

- Make sure pupil is not teased or bullied.

- Be alert for signs of anxiety or depression.

- Choose music to be played or listened to carefully.

Tourette Syndrome (UK) Association
PO Box 26149, Dunfermline KY12 7YU
Tel: 0845 458 1252 (Helpline)
Tel: 01383 629600 (Admin) Fax: 01383 629609
Email: enquiries@tsa.org.uk Website: http://www.tsa.org.uk

CHAPTER 4

The Inclusive Music Classroom

The physical state of the classroom is particularly important for some children, for example wheelchair users, pupils with visual impairments and those on the autistic spectrum. In this chapter we will consider the physical layout and attributes of the music room, from size and space to the furniture, equipment and display.

We will bear in mind all pupils, including those with special educational needs. This will be a classroom where all kinds of learners can learn and get along together. In the real world, we have to work within the limitations of the rooms and resources available to us and within the constraints of various budgets. Part 4 of the Disability Discrimination Act 1995 does not require schools to make physical alterations to improve access to school buildings as these longer-term strategic changes will be achieved through LEA planning duties. There are, however, adaptations that can be made relatively easily and cheaply and it is these that we will explore.

The position of the music department within the school building may not be negotiable, but it is worth mentioning that it should be situated where lessons can go on – unimpeded – all school day long, all year round, whatever other activities are happening within the school. Where music departments have their rooms close to the school hall in order to facilitate performances such as school concerts and assembly contributions, they inevitably find themselves also close to the exam room [which is also the school hall] and unable to make any noise for a significant amount of time.

Ideally the music department should be a suite of soundproof carpeted rooms, one of which can be used as a recording studio. It should be located on the ground floor, possibly next to the drama studio, as part of a Performing Arts suite.

Between each room in the music suite there should be triple-glazed glass/perspex (studio quality) windows, with vertical blinds for occasional privacy. If space is at a premium, you could consider using moveable walls to accommodate a large audience (for example, two year groups). The biggest room might contain a low stage, with a ramp up from both sides. There should be one or two large teaching rooms, a large performance room, a private, staff-only

Quiet please, there's an exam going on next door.

office, and several smaller store cupboards and practice rooms. One of these smaller rooms can double as a retreat or 'time-out' room, a quiet space where pupils can work individually or in a pair. This room should be big enough for a wheelchair and one or two pupils, and an adult. The door should have a window so that the teacher can monitor the pupils' work even when the door is closed.

Furniture

At least some of the desks and tables should be adjustable and arranged in a way which allows for easy movement around the room. Stools are a good seating option, and make space for pupils who use wheelchairs, crutches or other mobility aids. However, some pupils with motor co-ordination difficulties will need the security of a chair back. Some music departments organise different zones, such as writing/listening areas and keyboards areas.

Arrangements should be made with the cleaning staff to keep the tables graffiti-free. A clean and pleasant environment makes it easier to maintain high standards of both work and behaviour.

Instruments

There should be enough rooms/space to leave drum-kits, steel pans and keyboards set up and in place. Violins, violas, and all brass and woodwind instruments should be stored in their cases. Guitars, cellos and double basses may be in cases, or safely put in custom-made racks. Glockenspiels and xylophones, etc. should be in neat rows on shelves. Untuned small percussion should be in trolleys or boxes. Congas and timbales etc. should be available to use, i.e. not cased up all the time, but put discreetly to one side. Decks are best set up in a locked studio.

In general, the more delicate and the smaller the instrument the more it needs to be stored in a case when not being played. Drum-kits should always be set up, and one should always be set up left-handed. Percussion instruments in particular are prone to people tapping them as they pass (this includes staff). Sticks and beaters need to be kept to one side in boxes. Removable glockenspiel notes are a nightmare and only advisable if the teacher desperately likes the flexibility. Far better to have chimes bars if you need to hand out less notes.

Personal belongings

It is useful to have coat racks in the main teaching room: most pupils like to keep their coats in sight and this allows them to be stored tidily. Providing a safe place for bags also avoids cluttering up the teaching area and minimises the risk of anyone tripping over.

There should be a no-go area around the teacher's desk. The central controls to turn the keyboards on and off, and also the sound systems and video, will be here. This is where the teacher can look after people's personal possessions. The keyboard wires and the headphone splitters can also be kept here. Here too should be all the pens and pencils. No lesson should ever be held up because a child has not got a pen, and the once-a-week music lesson is not the place to fight for a child's stationery responsibilities.

Technical support

Music departments benefit considerably from having allocated to them two or three hours a week of technician time. This person can check over and repair the headphones, the keyboards etc. on a weekly basis. They should tune the guitars and all other stringed instruments and replace worn strings. How much lesson time is lost both by peripatetic teachers and by classroom teachers in tuning up instruments, or looking round for working headphones? Have spare keyboard electrical leads available so that no keyboards are ever out of action.

The technician should put the keys back on the xylophones and glockenspiels. S/he should generally stack and tidy, bin broken items and advise on replacements. A notebook is a useful way for the technician to pass on information about breakages or equipment that needs replacing.

Where there are good links with the local community, it may be possible to find a parent (or grandparent) and/or governor who has some spare time and would be only too pleased to help out in the role of volunteer assistant. In such cases, CRB checks need to be made for security reasons, and some time invested in 'training'. In the best circumstances however, such 'helpers' can be invaluable – remember to show appropriate appreciation!

Display

Display should:

- be relevant

- be interesting

- be up-to-date

- be well-presented and

- include children's own work

There should be key words, placed in some sort of logical order, on a wall or a board or on a screen. They could be changed monthly, weekly, daily or even, if it makes the difference that the teacher needs, for each lesson. Indeed, the latter would suit children with hearing impairments or learning difficulties as they would benefit from having available additional visual information linked to the lesson. Be aware that for pupils with autistic spectrum disorder, busy, colourful displays can prove over-stimulating; being allowed to sit near to or facing a plain wall can help them to remain focused on the lesson.

Music can reflect children's own culture and society and classroom displays can be a place to showcase their favourite artists. Apart from obviously being an opportunity to display musicians and instruments from different ethnic minorities, and to portray women and girls in a positive way, the wall display is where we can put on show artists with disabilities. If the disability is not obvious, an explanatory sentence can make it so.

Give consideration to the height of displays – wheelchair users will have a lower eye-level than their peers, and make sure that lettering is as big and bold as possible so that pupils with less than perfect vision can still read it. Using a digital camera to photograph pupils playing instruments and engaged in different activities can help to produce colourful and interesting displays that are very relevant and immediate. Photographs can also be effective in the production of 'visual instructions' – particularly useful for hearing-impaired and autistic students. If you use photographs, you must ensure that, if the rooms or corridors that they are displayed in are used by the public, permission is obtained from parents or carers.

Instruments and equipment

In this section, we list all the instruments you would need for including pupils with special educational needs. For pupils with physical disabilities and limited motor skills, there are many specialised pieces of equipment, devised and pioneered by such organisations as the Drake Music Project.

Pupils often prefer the instruments that give them appropriate 'street cred' and in order to avoid competition for 'the best' of anything, it can be advisable to have all the same keyboards, all the same guitars, all the same drum-kits, and a large number of all the same untuned percussion.

But the piece of equipment that will reach just about everybody is the microphone!

Singing, vocals, microphones and karaoke

The voice is the most natural musical tool/instrument, yet it renders the user most vulnerable. The recent upsurge in interest in pop singing and the many television competitions for singers have enthused unprecedented numbers of pupils for the voice. The microphone brings power effortlessly to the voice as volume, and, of course, with volume comes personal power.

Pupils with learning and behavioural difficulties

For pupils with BESD or MLD the microphone offers power and street cred.
I have seen a music teacher in Leeds take a class of pupils, mostly girls with no self-esteem and absolutely no social graces, and have them as putty in his hands as they queued up to take their turn with the karaoke. And these very same pupils later that term took solo spots in an evening production of 'Grease'.

In one Leeds school pupils, including some with Down's Syndrome always finish their music lessons off with a karaoke type performance, taking turns to hold a microphone and sing along with their favourite pop song.

Pupils with dyslexia, dyscalculia and dyspraxia, as long as they do not feel uncomfortable about their voice, will be liberated by singing and should achieve well.

Pupils with physical difficulties

With an effects unit, pupils with physical difficulties can create satisfying and imaginative musical sounds. With a more mainstream effects unit, pupils can play about with the sounds that their own voices create.

Pupils with sensory impairments

Pupils who are hearing impaired should be empowered by the amplified sound of their own voice. Microphones will not be effective with the profoundly deaf unless they can feel the vibrations of the amplifier, and this is best achieved by both pupil and amplifier standing on a sounding board (or nicely resonant wooden floor).

Pupils with communication difficulties

For pupils who stammer or who have Tourette's Syndrome singing can be truly liberating, as it usually transcends the difficulties they encounter in speech.

Drum-kits

It is a good idea to have at least three drum-kits if possible, with one permanently set up for left-handed players. One set should always be ready for the drummers to play along with the school's band, be it rock, jazz or steel.

> Daniel was a pupil whose father was a professional drummer, and whose intended high school had closed before he was old enough to go to it. Consequently he lived miles from anyone else in his class, and wasn't particularly happy at school. His one consolation was his drum-kit lessons with the world's greatest drum-kit 'peri'. Everybody expected him to follow his father's footsteps and be a professional musician. One day the headteacher called him out of lessons at a moment's notice to stand in for the rock band's regular drummer who was ill. The local MP was paying a visit, with the photographers in tow. Alas, the regular drummer was right-handed. Daniel was not. Daniel was just about to swap the snare and the hi-hat over when the head stopped him. 'No time for that', he called, 'Just play'. The following discussion between head and pupil cannot be recorded here. Daniel spent three days at home. The episode ended in no more drum-kit lessons and no musical career.

Pupils with learning and behavioural difficulties

For pupils with MLD and with BESD the drum-kit is often *the* instrument. It has associations of power, and of masculinity, and it has great street cred. Often boys resent girls being good at the drum-kit, and they try to 'psyche them out' of playing well. Girls with emotional problems often, in our experience, love learning to play the drum-kit, and will totally discard their poor behaviour long enough to learn this instrument. Boys with BESD, however, need carefully planned 5–10 minutes learning bursts, or it can be quite counter-productive, as they vent their frustration at their very-quickly realised incompetence on the drums.

Pupils with physical difficulties

For pupils with PMLD, Cerebral Palsy and other physical difficulties staff should arrange and adjust the various pieces of the drum-kit to enable pupils to play.

Pupils with sensory impairments

For pupils who are deaf or who are hearing impaired drum-kits, and in fact all other drums, have the vibro-tactile element. They can develop and improve their sense of rhythm through copying. Pupils get feedback from the feeling of the vibrations and also visually, especially if they are working with a partner who is on another kit.

For the pupils who are visually-impaired staff should approach drum-kits with great care. They can be instantly very loud, and unless the pupil is forewarned, the noise can be terrifying.

Pupils with communication difficulties

For pupils with Autism and Asperger's Syndrome it's hard to generalise about the drum-kit. They may be intrigued by the patterns that can be created by the way that they are played or by the way the kit is set up. When pupils develop a liking for drums, they may become obsessive about them – it will be important to ensure that they understand about having to take turns.

Guitars

For class guitar teaching the traditional Spanish guitar is best. The nylon strings are gentler on the beginners' finger tips, and the slightly wider necks are easier to fit your fingers onto, rather than the thinner Jumbo steel string and twelve-string guitars. For those forming their own rock bands and studying with the peripatetic tutors, the school will need some electric guitars including at least one bass guitar. Always be sure to string at least one guitar left-handed. Guitars should always have cases, preferably hard ones. This will help them stay in tune as well as protect them.

Pupils with learning and behaviour difficulties

The guitar, like the drum-kit, is usually perceived to be 'cool', and this is motivating for these pupils. With carefully planned introductory lessons, using single-finger chords and well-known pop songs (the theme from 'Titanic' can get on your nerves after eight years though!), pupils can be very successful.

Beginners on electric guitars can sound awful and they make a lot of noise. Use headphones with amps, and only allow pupils to have the jack leads when they have something to perform to the rest of the class.

Pupils with BESD are often quite able, with naturally good fine motor skills; they may take quite easily to playing melody lines on guitar.

With open tuning, pupils with Down's Syndrome, MLD and SLD can all make meaningful sounds, though variable progress, on a guitar.

Pupils with physical difficulties

Many pupils with seriously restricted or unpredictable movement – e.g. those with Cerebral Palsy like the feel of the sound of an acoustic guitar. This can be made possible by placing the instruments flat on their wheelchair table or other surface. The pupil can then strum the strings while someone else changes the chords. Or they could use open tuning and share the chords out between several pupils.

If it is the sound of the strings that is the 'turn-on' then the somewhat unfashionable autoharp might be a good idea here. It is much easier for the helper to change chords on an autoharp than on a guitar.

Bass guitars are very good for pupils with limited hand and finger movement. Pupils with only one arm or hand need open tuning.

Pupils with sensory impairment

For pupils who are deaf and hearing impaired the guitar has plus and minus features. The acoustic guitar can be felt rather than heard, but for those with some hearing, an electric guitar may be better. Each pupil would be best with their own amp near to them (or headphones) so they can clearly detect what they are playing. An electro acoustic would seem to be the best of both worlds.

Guitars are ideal for pupils who are visually impaired. Because they hold the instrument to themselves, once they have learnt the basics, they will instantly know where everything is, and they don't have to rely upon anyone else to set the equipment up. Any hardening of the finger tips should not affect the player's ability to read Braille, as this is read further down the finger on the pads just below the tips.

Pupils with multi-sensory impairment will have a mixture of the above. The teacher and support staff should experiment to see how well they would get on with a guitar.

Pupils with communication problems

Pupils who are autistic or have Asperger's Syndrome may well take to this, enjoying the sense of patterns and structure which playing chords and tunes on the guitar gives. Some with sensitive hearing may prefer the quieter sound of the acoustic guitar.

Keyboards (and the piano)

There are multitudes of types of electronic keyboards out there in the shops, and, unfortunately, even more lying around in our schools. Their best features are also their worst features: endless switches and dials that prevent a person from playing a melody or constructing a chord or keeping time for themselves.

What a Head of Music would buy if they were starting from scratch, and if money were no object, would probably be different from the reality. And the reality is, too often, the worst possible scenario: lots of different types of keyboards, some not working or missing keys; headphones broken, or working in only one ear. (Fortunately there are firms which specialise in return-of-post headphone repairs, and they can transform the music teacher's life).

There is also the Music Laboratory invented by Nicholas Haines. This is a wonderful way of giving individual attention to the biggest number of pupils in any one session. (See appendices for details.)

Pupils with learning and behavioural difficulties

Pupils with learning difficulties enjoy and benefit from experimenting with the sounds made by a keyboard. For these pupils, marking either note names, scales or chords with letters or colours is probably necessary. Playing pentatonic tunes on just the black notes is a good way to give these pupils a sense of achievement.

When including pupils with BESD, if the teacher systematically insists on the whole class using headphones, and keeps a wary eye on the pupils with attention and behaviour problems, then keyboards can be the way through to these pupils working, learning and playing for its own sake. With no one to show off to, no one to disrupt, they will eventually get bored of listening to the preset tunes, and start to teach themselves. With headphone splitters the teacher can quickly reward those who are working and give them little bursts of attention. Splitters again are good for these pupils to get used to co-operating and working in pairs.

Touch sensitivity can spoil the performance for pupils with poor motor skills, and this will irritate pupils with emotional problems. (It is best to buy keyboards that can turn this facility on and off.) Everybody loves all the things that the keyboards can do. With all the latest technical developments there should be enough to challenge and absorb all pupils, including those with behaviour difficulties.

If there is a real piano in the room the pupils with BESD will gravitate towards it. They often say that they really like the sound better, and this may be true, but the pupil cannot control the volume or use headphones and so other pupils will be distracted. The piano should be for the teacher's use only in general music lessons. Pupils who are taking piano lessons can use it at pre-arranged times.

In order to check out the pupil's interest in a piano you could let them use the one in the empty practice room (if you have one); and see if they stay as long on that as they do the one in the main teaching room.

Pupils with physical disabilities

For pupils with Cerebral Palsy you can get key guards and switch guards. These are fitted over the keyboard to enable a pupil with poor muscle tone to avoid playing unwanted notes and rhythms. Note clusters are easier to play than individual notes. Cubase is a good programme to use for pupils with CP if they want to record a keyboard piece.

Some pupils with CP may have good foot control – placing the keyboard on the floor and taking off the pupils shoes and socks can be amazingly liberating for the pupil and enable them to join in real time in an ensemble piece.

Pupils with communication difficulties

For many pupils with Asperger's Syndrome/Autism there is something about the keyboard (including piano and organ) which fascinates. This does not apply to all, but if they are interested then they can be obsessive, and this can become a problem when it comes to finishing a session.

They may wish to audition all the sounds within the keyboard, and may well have certain playing routines which they do each time they play – these may be more about the patterns created than about the sound. Some pupils with ASD find wearing headphones a frightening or uncomfortable experience. Allow the student to hold the headphones first and put them on for themselves when they feel comfortable with the idea.

Pupils with severe autism often put their hands over their ears when any music is played. This may not be because it is too loud – it may just be that the sound was unexpected and they are giving themselves time to come to terms with it.

Do not be put off by the hands over the ears – or even adverse reactions. With careful management the pupil may learn to get used to new sounds and may actually enjoy them in time.

The pupils on the autistic spectrum often love the pure acoustic sounds of a real piano. Where students seem to be locked away in their own worlds, music can be the interface that makes the breakthrough, and the instruments with their pure acoustic sounds are more likely to help them do it. There may also be something about the precise [chromatic] layout of the notes that may make a piano lend itself to being easily mastered and understood/enjoyed by the pupil with autism.

Pupils with sensory impairments

There is very little vibration for a profoundly deaf pupil to feel with a keyboard. If it is connected to an amp and the speakers placed near to the pupil, preferably in a room with a resonant floor or on a sounding board, then some use may be made of them. Pupils with some hearing may be able to turn them up enough to benefit from them.

A grand piano is probably the best solution for pupils who are deaf. If they can be around the piano actually touching the wood then they will get a real feeling for the sound. A wooden floor will make this even better with the vibrations being felt through the feet.

In his later and deafer years Beethoven, whenever he was at the piano playing or composing, would hold a piece of wood in his mouth which led down onto the soundboard, and in this way he could feel what he was playing.

Pupils who are hearing impaired do manage to learn to play the piano sometimes to a very high level – e.g. pianist Julia Shirabe from Japan. She gained a degree in Music as did Paul Whittaker (specialising on the organ), now from Music and the Deaf.

For pupils with PMLD, developing the hand control to press down a group of notes on the keyboard may be a huge achievement.

Steel pans

Originally from Trinidad, steel pans are becoming increasingly more popular in Britain and Europe, both as a teaching and as a performance instrument. With the right combination of teaching methods steel pans are the ultimate inclusive teaching instrument, and not just for pupils with SEN.

Steel pans comprise various basic instruments, each with a different lay-out, range of pitch and number of notes on each 'pan'. If the school intends to run a band and play gigs, then they must buy cases and instruct the pupils in care and carrying.

Pupils with learning and behavioural difficulties

Although a steel pan is and can be an individual instrument, like the gamelan, it is as a whole band/class that it is learnt and played. Like chime bars and other tuned percussion instruments, it is particularly suited to colour coding of chords. This makes teaching as a band very easy, because all of the class are involved all the time.

The disadvantages of steel pans for these pupils is that they can easily be damaged and knocked out of tune, and tuners are expensive and still in short supply in Britain. They are loud and you can't turn them off. Having said that, it is very easy to get a very satisfying sound very quickly. And pupils depend on others to create this satisfying sound, so they soon realise that it is in their own interest to co-operate with others.

One great advantage that steel pans have, over just about every other instrument, is that they are freestanding. Pupils stand to play them. They do not need to lose their independence or freedom of action by having to hold or support the instrument. Thus the pan in no way threatens or compromises the pupil's security or dignity.

Pupils with physical difficulties

There are already professional wheelchair-using steel pan players. They use specially adapted pan stands that clip on to the wheelchair. For others there are two-note single bass pans (with 1sts and 5ths on them) with large surface areas. These would be very suitable for pupils with poor motor skills.

Pupils with sensory impairments

The piercing metal sounds may get through to most pupils with HI, and the deaf pupils would get vibrations from the big bass pans if both the pans and themselves were standing on resonant boards.

For pupils who are blind or visually impaired steel pans should present very few problems as long as the pupil plays the same individual instrument each time (being hand-made, there are slight variations). These pupils are best steered to the singles, either soprano/tenor pans or single seconds, single guitars etc. Pans each have a small compact surface area, and each note is big enough to give the player between 5 and 10cm leeway on the larger notes of a soprano/tenor pan and more on the lower-pitched pans.

Steel pans would not be so easy for pupils with MSI. You can't hold the pans to play them as that dampens the sound.

Pupils with communication difficulties

Give pupils with autistic spectrum disorders opportunities to experiment on the steel pans individually before they are expected to work as part of a group.

Chime Bars, glockenspiels and xylophones

If your vision of chime bars consists of an assortment of blue plastic rolls with rotting rubber and rusty pins, put it to one side, and get out the Percussion Plus catalogue. The catalogue includes a range of robust, 'child proof' instruments that allow pupils to enjoy playing without being anxious about breakages. For preference choose alto-pitched instruments.

Pupils with learning and behavioural difficulties

Chime bars allow pupils to physically move pitch around and experiment with it. Pupils with Down's Syndrome and similar learning difficulties need only be given their own note, and they will always make a satisfying contribution to the pieces played as ensembles. Pupils with limited motor skills can have just the one note to look for and concentrate on. Over time, and when they are ready, each pupil can be given more notes.

The best glockenspiels are those that look like regular keyboards with white naturals and black sharps and flats, and have notes the same size as piano keys. For pupils with SLD there is a one octave diatonic glockenspiel (C – C with only white notes).

Pupils with physical difficulties

Chime bars come in various sizes and can easily be positioned so that pupils with little control over their movements can get to them. It is also possible to attach a beater to the wrist of a pupil who finds it hard to grip.

Pupils with sensory impairments

Pupils who are deaf or hearing impaired can enjoy playing chime bars even though the sound may need to be felt rather than heard. It is helpful to give a visual idea of the relative pitches.

Wooden Tone Bars are specially designed for pitch work with deaf pupils. The sound can be felt by touching the sides and is easier to hear. It dies away quickly (thus avoiding the confusion of sounds building up) and they have less harmonic confusion than instruments with metal sounds.

Chime bars and tone bars are particularly suitable for pupils with visual impairments; they are held securely in the hand and can be used independently in ensemble playing.

Pupils with communication difficulties

These are extremely accessible instruments for these pupils.

Orchestral instruments

All pupils need to be given the opportunity to try to play the different orchestral instruments as well as to hear them. Teachers should be careful that pupils with learning difficulties observe basic hygiene rules and not exchange mouthpieces when playing woodwind and brass instruments.

Pupils with learning and behavioural difficulties

Short taster sessions on these instruments will help develop an appreciation for the skills needed to play orchestral instruments. However, it would be a brave pupil with behaviour problems who carried his or her violin home through the inner-city streets.

On the other hand, pupils with MLD will enjoy trying to play these familiar-shaped instruments, and will often persevere with them and achieve more than expected.

Pupils with physical difficulties

Pupils with physical difficulties (including PMLD) should not be denied the pleasure of attempting to play these instruments.

> There was once a boy whose family thought he was frightened of musical instruments because he screamed whenever he saw them. One day the classroom assistant gave him a violin bow to hold, and together they stroked the instrument's strings. The boy stopped screaming and started smiling. It was not fear, his family realised, but frustration at not being able to touch and play the desired object.

Pupils with sensory impairments

Pupils who are deaf or hearing impaired will enjoy the vibro-tactile experience of the orchestral instruments, especially the low-pitched strings: cellos and double basses.

> The local string trio were visiting a school. The cellist was slightly alarmed when a deaf boy with SLD threw himself at her feet and lay on the floor before her, but she kept her nerve and went on playing, and as she did, the boy began taking in the vibrations and kicking the floor in time with the music.

Pupils who are blind or visually impaired will be able to learn any instrument they choose. As this is an area in which they are very likely to succeed, if there are limited places for tasters, these pupils should be at the front of the queue. (See Sally Zimmerman's book published by RNIB on this.)

Pupils with communication difficulties

An individual pupil may take to an individual instrument. If everyone else is having a taster, so should they.

Untuned percussion

This will include the instruments of the Samba Band, and all the African instruments.

Pupils with learning and behavioural difficulties

Pupils with BESD may initially lack the self-discipline required to put in the silences and listen to instructions. However, with informed teaching, they can succeed.

Pupils with MLD should be taught how to hold and play these instruments correctly and not treat them as toys. Activities based on familiar rhythms, such as the pupils' own names or football chants, will enable all pupils to join in.

Pupils with SLD will succeed at and enjoy sessions with untuned percussion instruments.

Pupils with physical difficulties including PMLD

Each instrument presents its own particular problems and needs to be approached with an open mind. Teacher and pupil should explore different ways of holding and playing. Percussion Plus supply various untuned percussion instruments mounted on stands which allow pupils to play them without holding them.

Pupils with sensory impairments

Pupils who are hearing impaired may find that they cannot hear some instruments such as bells and shakers. They will prefer rain sticks and ocean drums because they will be able to feel and see them. Wood blocks and claves along with hand held drums produce sounds which seem to penetrate better than metallic sounds.

Pupils with communication difficulties

These instruments are ideal for working interactively with pupils with ASD on a one-to-one basis with their assistant or a fellow pupil (see the work on Musical Interaction by Wendy Prevezer). Pupils particularly enjoy playing the wooden clatterpillar, the rainsticks and ocean drums.

Other miscellaneous instruments

The Gamelan

Few schools currently own a Gamelan but it is an instrument which can benefit many pupils with special needs. It is, in effect, an orchestra of South East Asian tuned percussion instruments – much more than an 'instrument'. It is a whole way of playing which is ideal for ensemble work. In order to play you will need to visit or have a visit from your local specialist.

Pupils with learning and behavioural difficulties

The Gamelan is a good instrument for including pupils with BESD, as the sounds are calming and all pupils are fully involved. However, if an outside tutor is leading the session, it will be important for him/her to be given information about children in the class who have SEN. The tutor should be experienced in behaviour management. Pupils with MLD/SLD will be able to participate in the Gamelan activity and this involvement will support their musical progress.

Pupils with physical difficulties

The individual notes can be placed on a wheelchair tray; the pupil can sit next to the large suspended gongs.

Pupils with sensory impairments

Pupils who are deaf or hearing impaired enjoy working in an ensemble and benefit from the Gamelan experience. However they may play the instruments too hard and knock them out of tune, and they may find it difficult to hear clearly with so many harmonics being present.

Pupils who are blind or visually impaired will enjoy the wonderful patterns made by the harmonics.

Pupils with communication difficulties

Pupils who have Semantic Pragmatic Language Disorder may enjoy the ensemble.

Pupils who are Autistic or who have Asperger's Syndrome may enjoy the precise number patterns, based on a count of eight, which are needed to play the Gamelan properly. Again the instructor will need knowledge of working with these pupils.

Sitars, tablas, harmoniums, and dhol

These South East Asian Instruments are becoming more popular in mainstream schools. Visually very exiting, their only drawback at concerts is the length of each piece. They require a high degree of skill to play well and are quite delicate. They will be very suitable for pupils who are blind and visually impaired.

Hand chimes and bell plates

These are particularly suitable for pupils with poor motor skills, especially the newly available bell paltes.

Boom whackers

These are hollow plastic pipes tuned to the notes of a scale and can be used successfully with virtually anybody. Their strength is their simplicity.

Autoharp

This rather old fashioned instrument may appeal to some pupils, especially those with poor motor skills and those who can't cope with loud noises.

Singing bowls

These create calming sounds that will benefit pupils with BESD and MLD and help the latter to develop good motor skills.

Ocarinas

Pupils who are deaf and hearing impaired may manage them even though they sometimes have problems blowing. Ocarinas are best played using the notation devised by The Ocarina Workshop. This graphic system also has great appeal for pupils who are autistic or have Asperger's Syndrome.

Technology

Computers open up so many possibilities and yet they can disempower pupils from the live scene by removing them from all human contact. They should be used for all the fabulous doors they open, but watch out for the doors they close.

ICT helps pupils develop musical skills and their knowledge and understanding of music in all its forms. It acts as a tool and a distinctive medium of musical expression and pupils can use ICT to:

- make and explore sounds

- record for different purposes

- structure, compose and perform music

- access information about music and musical instruments (see www.classicsforkids.com for a music dictionary with illustrations and audio examples)

- understand musical processes

At the time of writing, there is a host of new developments on the music technology front. The international technology exhibition *BETT*, which is hosted at Olympia, London, every January provides an excellent opportunity for music teachers to explore new developments such as the interactive music education system *Gigajam*. Some of the software developed for the primary sector is also worth exploring for KS 3 pupils with SEN, incuding the *Music Toolkit* that encourages pupils to investigate a range of musical concepts.

Soundbeam (originally developed as a therapeutic tool) has been recognised as having enormous potential in the music classroom. The 'virtual keyboard' can be just that, or it can be a set of strings, a drum-kit or a producer of natural sounds such as birdsong. The machine functions as an information processor which translates movement into signals which are understood by electronic instruments, so that pupils can 'play' an instrument merely by moving a hand, or foot. Key issues such as timing, pitch and rhythm are just as important to a *Soundbeam* player as to any instrumentalist, and skills of concentration are essential when playing as part of a group.

Pupils with BESD and MLD

Computers motivate pupils with BESD and MLD brilliantly and behaviour always improves when students are engrossed in programs such as *Band in a Box* and *E-Jay*.

Pupils with physical difficulties

Using feet is a good way for some pupils to use a mixing desk – I have seen a young man with Cerebral Palsy run the mixing desk for a whole show with all the equipment spread out along the floor, i.e. professional mixing desk, computer running Cubase, and keyboard. His wheelchair enabled him to move along from one piece of equipment to another (details are available from the Drake Music Project and Share Music).

Switches are on-off buttons which are interfaces between the pupil and all that the technological outside world has to offer. Switches have revolutionised the role of a pupil with physical difficulties in the music group. (For suppliers see Appendix 1.)

The music teacher can use the pupil's personal switch to connect up to various pieces of ICT equipment in order for them to create meaningful musical sounds. There are various pieces of equipment on the market which allow this. They are principally:

- Midi Creator

- EMS Sound Beam

These can give the pupil access to any sound that can be found within Sound Module, Midi Keyboard or Sampler. The only limitations are those of the pupil's imagination and the person operating the equipment. With these switches a pupil can choose a sound and play single notes, chords, scales, groups of notes, etc.

If this is then connected via Midi to a computer with a sequencer these sounds can be recorded onto disk. They can be in real time or put in using step time and then speeded up according to the pupil's wishes.

The most basic and the most important switch is the Big Mack. This records a few snatches of sound and can be pressed by the pupil or linked to their own switch, enabling them to contribute to the music lesson.

The more complex version of this is the Quintet, which as its name suggests is a series of five switches which can play musical phrases or fragments.

Computers themselves can do many wonderful things but making their world available to pupils with physical difficulties has only been possible by using the following:

- step time within Cubase (or other sequencer)

- using a tracker ball rather than a mouse – much easier to control

- splitting up the functions of the mouse to enable a switch user to move around the screen

- the E-Scape program produced by The Drake Music Project

For pupils with PMLD the speakers need to be close to the players ears so that they can connect the sounds that they create with the sounds that they hear.

Pupils with sensory impairment

For pupils who are hearing impaired computers are probably not the best use of their time in the music session.

For Pupils who are blind and visually impaired *Cakewalk* is one of the best sequencer options because it can operate on keyboard commands only. Adding a screen reader such as Jaws is essential. This is available from the RNIB online shop.

Pupils with communication difficulties

Pupils with ASD or Asperger's Syndrome are often skilled and enthusiastic users of computers but may also be obsessive about their use. If other pupils are using computers in the music lesson, the student with ASD may find it difficult to concentrate on anything else. Plan separate music technology lessons for classes that include pupils with ASD so that they are able to develop both the practical and technological skills of music.

CHAPTER 5

Teaching and Learning Styles

In this chapter we outline various learning styles and comment on them briefly, discussing ways in which they are already in use, and how pupils with SEN benefit when teachers plan lessons to accommodate their particular learning styles. Then we will consider teaching methods; how rules and routines can be used to support pupils with SEN. We will also consider, but only briefly, behaviour management.

We will consider six learning styles which have particular relevance to the music classroom: aural, visual, kinaesthetic, learning from notation, theoretical and multi-sensory.

Aural: students listen and sing or play from hearing only. This method of learning suits people with perfect or perfect relative pitch; they may be limited in technical skills. For the aurally inclined deaf pupil, you must use acoustic instruments, preferably, but not exclusively, with lower frequencies.

Visual: students watch somebody demonstrate playing. Most tutor books have pictures of hand and finger positions. This method would not suit visually impaired or dyslexic pupils but is ideal for those who see in pictures, such as the pupils with autism who could possibly memorise a long sequence of shapes. Kodály's hand signs figure in this style of teaching and learning.

Hand signs are a way of giving a physical placement for a vocal pitch. The low 'Doh' begins at your midsection. Each pitch is then above the previous one. Thus, you have the hand signs going up when the pitch goes up. The upper 'Doh' is at eye level.

La   Soh   Me

Notation: is where music is represented in symbols. This could be either conventional western notation, graphic notation, letters, piano roll or tablature etc. Players translate notes on paper into meaningful sound. This is obviously difficult for blind and visually impaired pupils (although Braille and enlarged score may be useful for some, and eliminate the visually impaired pupil's dependence on others). Some pupils with dyslexia and dyscalculia may prefer musical notation to reading ordinary text, and pupils with dyslexia often prefer numbers to letters for the notes of a scale (or key).

Kinaesthetic: is where you learn by feeling the movement of the music with your body. People with poor motor skills and co-ordination will find this difficult, but will benefit greatly from clapping, stamping feet and dancing, actions useful for rhythm work, tempo and phrasing. Dalcroze introduced movement to conservatoire students as a way of introducing musical elements.

Theory: is where a student works out what chord or note is likely to come next by what they have learnt theoretically. Using chords in a key would come into this, and it would particularly suit deaf and hearing impaired pupils and those who are blind and visually impaired.

Multi-sensory: is where pupils use all of their senses to learn about music. As the teacher, you will create 'theatre in the classroom'; that is using music, lights, smells, touch and taste, which all create atmospheres, and heightening of a pupil's awareness of their surrounding and the task in hand.

Everybody tends to implement more than one style as they learn. For example, someone may like to see the notes in front of them, but have the melody sung or played to them beforehand as well. The so-called aural tradition is also very visual: folk guitarists and fiddle-players will watch as much as listen; and steel pan players traditionally show each other what to do. If a person is using theory to work out the notes and chords to a song they will also be listening for the same.

Even before including pupils with SEN in the class, the music teacher is already accommodating pupils' different learning needs. One pupil will be saying 'Show me'; one pupil will be demanding the written music; another will need a different type of notation (maybe asking for the letters to be written under the notes); another may need to clap out a phrase of music before they are able to play it on their chosen instrument. Guitarists with dyslexia will probably prefer tablature over western notation.

When you include pupils in the class with different forms of SEN you will start to consider what is the best learning style for each individual, and how you, the teacher, can support them in this. You may initially expect, for example, a deaf person to prefer a visual method of learning (signing and Kodály) and to be happy with notation, but you shouldn't be surprised by the broken moulds. A deaf pupil may prefer to learn kinaesthetically. (Always ask the deaf pupil what and if s/he can hear.)

Notations in relation to SEN

Notation was used originally as an aide-memoir to show the direction of the melody. Gradually colours and shapes were introduced and over the centuries the sophisticated system that is western notation evolved.

Along with notation a curious degree of musical snobbery has arisen. Notation is seen as the only way to approach western music, while learning aurally seems acceptable for jazz, folk and world music. Between them, these two methods seem to exclude as many players as they include.

Many teachers are adamant that they are teaching notation during lessons, yet a quick look around the classroom will tell you that besides having the piece of music in front of them, pupils are writing letter names under the 'dots', demanding to hear how each section is played, and asking teachers to show them what to do.

Written notations

1. Conventional western/staff notation with its different clefs

This might appeal to pupils with Asperger's Syndrome, and some pupils with reading difficulties may find music notations, which have a graphic element, more accessible than the written word.

2. Guitar tablature

This way of reading often suits pupils with dyslexia (see Appendix 1: Oglethorpe).

3. Guitar chord boxes

This is excellent for people with under-developed reading skills.

4. Braille

It is liberating to give the pupil a measure of independence. However, it is bulky and quite complex. This could be western notation made difficult (see Appendix 1: RNIB, Ockleford).

5. Foxwood Songsheets

These were designed specifically for including pupils with behaviour problems and some learning difficulties in mainstream classes (see Appendix 1).

6. Ocarina diagrams

These are like guitar boxes (see Ocarina Workshop materials, (Appendix 1: Ocarina Workshop).

7. Piano tablature

This is useful for pupils who find the concept of left to right when the pitch goes up and down difficult to understand. This is particularly true for pupils with dyslexia. This is a visual notation with a layout related to the instrument, with lines going up and down (See Oglethorpe reference in Appendix 1).

8. Graphic notation

This fits in well with the PECs system that is often used by pupils with ASD. It appeals to pupils who have a hearing impairment or learning difficulties because it offers additional visual cues.

9. Tactile scores

Similar to graphic notation but more suited to pupils who have a visual impairment. (see Appendix 1: RNIB, Ockleford).

Teaching methods

Given all these different ways of learning, the classroom teacher will need to place the emphasis on differentiation in order to achieve effective inclusion. This will mean accommodating as many learning styles as possible in your teaching approaches.

If you are teaching the pupils to play a song:

- Play a version of the song to them, either live yourself or a recording on CD/tape/minidisk etc., or preferably do both.

- Have a clearly-labelled folder/box with the score/notation in various formats (western notation, as letters – maybe Foxwood songsheets, Braille, enlarged, colour-coded chords).

- Ask them to clap out, sing the words, tune, rhythm of what is to be learnt.

'Don't worry about the theory Miss, just tell me what notes to play.'

- Go round showing each person what to do, which notes to play (watch out for the attention-seekers who don't really need you).

- Tell them that the notes will come from the song's key, so, if in G, for example, avoid F naturals, and only use F sharps.

- Tell them what notes to play.

Pupils usually employ a combination of learning styles, depending on the activity. Sometimes the style of learning that they most favour, e.g. notation, may be because of an unhappy experience with the aural tradition. They may, over time, return to the other style of learning, but need notation in the interim. Being told that you can only learn visually/aurally instruments such as folk guitar or steel pans is putting off pupils in droves from learning and succeeding on those instruments.

Rules and routines

Rules and routines are essential in the inclusive music lesson. Some children have chaotic lives outside school and while they might initially fight against the routines and rules within the classroom, they usually come to accept them and value the security they give.

However, how a teacher deals with each individual's anti-social and attention-seeking behaviour depends on your understanding of the causes and of the most appropriate treatment for the individual. In some schools, the Behaviour Support Unit gives all heads of department a set of individual behaviour plans, which outline probable behaviour and the best solutions. Alison, for example, may be asked to 'cool off for 5 minutes' if her temper gets the better of her in class, after which she will return and apologise. For a similar offence, the appropriate sanction for Haleema may be a phone call to her parents at home.

In some classes in some inner-city schools there may be a high number of pupils with challenging behaviour, and the music teacher may feel that the class is unmanageable. At this point the teacher may have to consider whether all the techniques in the world are ever going to get this class to work together. And of course this situation is particularly difficult in music lessons where there is care of equipment to consider and where listening and creation of moods is important.

Proper resourcing, especially of the human variety, can help, but so can good organisation and appropriate structuring of lessons. Every lesson should be a well-organised lesson with a clear beginning (starter), middle and ending (plenary/performance), and before they leave the room, the pupils should be back sitting down at their desks with their work collected in.

The pupils should have a clear idea of what they are to study. It's a good idea to have the lesson title and aim displayed on a flip-chart or whiteboard. We also recommend that pupils make a note in their music folders and their planners of the aims and outcomes (intended and otherwise). (See CD for suggested record sheets.)

In one school all the music staff do warm-ups and cool-downs by singing and chanting the register. The teacher will sing mostly first names but when he/she sings first and second names the pupil has to stand up and sing/chant their full name back.

Rules

The school's generic rules are usually displayed on the classroom wall and will often be augmented by specific rules for the music room (see Appendix 4 and CD).

Obviously, if a school's policy is to have all pupils standing up as a member of staff enters the room, the other pupils in the class will not object if the wheelchair user stays seated. However, this excludes the wheelchair user from the process. Either the school should consider changing this action to one that the wheelchair-users can comply with, e.g. sit up straight, or stop talking/communicating, or create a suitable equivalent action for the wheelchair-user.

Headphones

Many pupils hate the loss of control and worry about missing out on what's happening elsewhere. They feel vulnerable because they can neither see nor hear the rest of the class (this is a disadvantage of the 'surfaces round the room' approach). Others may have medical reasons for not being able to tolerate something on their head. Generally, however, since the advent of Walkmans and computers most pupils are used to headphones, so our advice is be strict but do watch out for the genuine refusniks.

Silence

One rule may be to be silent at times, for example when listening to a performance or to a recording. A pupil with, for example, Tourette's Syndrome may be unable to comply with the silence rule and the rest of the class must be sympathetic to his/her difficulty, and be accepting of the noises that are made involuntarily. One way to avoid this situation is for a group of pupils to listen to the recording on headphones, while the rest of the class are involved in other activities.

Literacy in music lessons

Information sheets, listening and activity sheets will be used from time to time and it is important to remember that some pupils will have limited literacy skills. If pupils are asked to research on the internet, they may well be faced with material that is difficult for them to read and understand. Pairing these students with a partner or 'buddy' who is a competent reader can help them to improve their reading skills generally, as well as ensure that they understand the content of any particular piece of musical information.

(The table opposite gives ideas for checking accessibility of written material.)

Making text accessible

Content

Can the core content be reduced/simplified?

(Remember that shorter sentences do not necessarily make for easier understanding).

Avoid passive constructions, e.g. 'The 1812 Overture was composed by Tchaikovsky'.

Instead, say 'composed the 1812 Overture'.

Are key points made clear?

Layout

Is the text spread out in manageable chunks?

Is text in clear print, e.g. word processed in a sans-serif font?

Are there line breaks in appropriate places?

Could there be more emphasis on key words?

Vocabulary

Can you provide a word bank for revision/introduction of core vocabulary? (See following page.)

Have you got a further vocabulary list for increasing the complexity of discussion and recording?

Are there any extra opportunities to practise using/reading/spelling the new vocabulary in a motivating context?

Do you provide opportunities to revisit essential vocabulary?

Do you offer creative as well as analytical activities for using vocabulary?

Reading

Could there be a simpler version?

Are there opportunities for more illustrations?

Would symbols add meaning? Could these be developed by the class?

Could content be tape recorded or videoed?

Can pupils work in pairs so that competent readers can help others?

Is text in electronic format? Text to speech software could be used.

Are there extra resources (CD-ROMs, reference books at a variety of levels, extension worksheets) for strugglers and quick finishers?

Word banks provide effective support for pupils with weak literacy skills and should be on display in the music room.

Sounds	**The Element of Music**	
		Pitch
Phrase		
	Duration	
		Pulse
	Rhythm	
Metre		
		Tempo
Timbre		
		Texture

There is little time for practising spellings in music lessons but learning key words and looking up meanings can provide useful homework activities. Tricky spellings may need to be taught quite carefully by the teacher or teaching assistant, e.g. 'rhythm'.

Rhythm

- look at it

- say it

- write it down

- cover it up and try to write it from memory

- if you get it wrong, look closely to see where you went wrong

- try again

Most people get the first and last letters correct – it is the middle of the word that proves difficult.

$$r \; - - - - \; m$$

$$h \, y \, t \, h$$

a mnemonic may help . . . e.g. **h**ave **y**ou **t**ried **h**opping
(The *Questions* Dictionary of Music is a useful resource: www.education-quest. com)

Writing

In order to get pupils to finish their written work it is quite common to tell them that they can't go onto the instruments until they have done it all. It is important to be able to distinguish between slow writers who can't help it and slow writers who won't get on with it. Some pupils with difficulties have to put in a great deal of effort to write even one sentence of legible, sensible text. Here you may pair pupils with writing difficulties or dyslexia with a writing partner or amanuensis, or allow them to work on a computer. There are many pupils with SEN whose writing, for all sorts of quite different reasons, may be under-developed for their age. Teachers need to remind themselves that music is not about writing, and have quite different and differentiated expectations of different pupils.

Stationery

It is sometimes difficult for some pupils with BESD to bring stationery to every lesson. Others, however, can bring bucket loads! Either way, this is not the lesson to make a public fuss about forgotten equipment, especially if forgetting a pen is the pupil's method of trying to get the wrong sort of attention. There are various ways round this problem, but the most important thing is for the teacher to have a pen or pencil ready for those without.

Mark on the register which pupils have borrowed pens, and collect them back in at the end of the lesson. Selling pens cheaply may be a good idea. Getting pupils to write their names on them and keep them in their music files is another idea. Whatever method you choose, you need to be very matter of fact about it, and reward all the others in some small way, possibly by congratulating them all for remembering equipment.

Behaviour management

When you include pupils with BESD in your music lessons you will need a good working understanding of behaviour management techniques. (There are some dos and don'ts on the CD.) Essentially you must be patient and firm, and the school needs to support you with quick-acting, consistently applied back up. Avoid raising your voice; don't make threats you can't carry out.

The teacher must make sure that the room contains as few temptations to disruption as possible. This is difficult in a music room, with so much equipment around, but the teacher can at least keep store cupboards closed or locked and keep the keys on him/her, and never leave them on a table or desk. The central switch for the keyboards should be not easily within reach of the pupils, and the teacher should build up a psychological barrier around the no-go area behind his/her desk.

Lastly, the teacher should apply praise statements and criticisms at a ratio of about 30 to 5 per 40-minute session. The praise should be honest, exact, evenly distributed and be for working quietly as well as for more overt achievements.

Ofsted guidance

There is clear guidance to Ofsted inspectors about what to look for in music lessons, and teachers may find the following points useful for evaluating their own practice:

Good teaching is rooted in:

- a good understanding of the subject, its examination syllabuses and programmes of study

- high expectations

- methods of teaching that cater for all pupils

Characteristics of good teaching in music include:

- Skilful use of pastiche to help pupils experience and understand a wide range of music in different styles and genres, from different cultures and historical periods;

- Pupils who are inspired and enthused by the teacher's ability to communicate ideas and express feelings and emotions through their own music

- The expectation that pupils will listen critically to music and use correct musical terminology when talking about it – and provide challenging opportunities for them to do so

- Pupils who are creative and imaginative in their music making

- Well-established, efficient and effective routines for the care, organisation and use of instruments which pupils adhere to

Examples of less than satisfactory teaching include instances where:

- Group work is the result of only one or two more competent or domineering pupils in the group

- Activities lack clear or sufficiently challenging objectives – for instance singing a particular song without an intention to improve diction or develop understanding of its structure; or writing notes on composers, drawing pictures of instruments

- Indiscriminate use of keyboards when acoustic instruments and percussion are more appropriate

- Use of worksheets that limit pupils' responses and constrain creativity

(Inspecting Music, Ofsted 2001: www.ofsted.gov.uk)

Summary

Music's great challenge as a class subject is that it all happens in real time. You can't go back and rub it out, or wait for someone to catch up. Unless you're encased in headphones everything that one pupil does affects everyone else. This is challenging enough for the average mainstream pupil, let alone for someone with hearing impairments or emotional problems.

Inclusion does not mean that everyone does the same thing, or is in the same room at the same time. Inclusion is about schools becoming secure, accepting, collaborating and stimulating communities in which everyone is valued (Booth *et al.* 2000).

The music teacher needs to have at her/his disposal a wide repertoire of teaching techniques and materials. S/he needs as much information as the SEN co-ordinator can provide in a form that is easy to assimilate. S/he needs to work in collaboration with teaching assistants in order to meet the needs of all pupils.

CHAPTER 6

Performing

Pupils arrive in your lessons with varying degrees of confidence. The teacher has a responsibility to set up a situation where all pupils feel comfortable and valued, where every note they sing and every note they play is valued.

Why perform?

Pupils with special needs should be encouraged to perform for the same reason as anyone else:

- to improve concentration

- provide a sense of achievement – a 'buzz'

- raise self esteem

- provide opportunities for self expression

- meet new challenges

- practise self discipline

- receive recognition (as applause)

In classroom performance you can afford to go wrong; on stage it's best not to. Classroom performance is more personal. Going on stage is also about all the extras: e.g. rehearsals, sense of audience, coping with nerves, appearance, choice of repertoire etc. Many pupils with special educational needs take part meaningfully in public performances and can actually step outside their special needs status, and take us all by surprise.

Whereas a pupil with severe learning difficulties may have nothing to offer the school's chances of gaining the maths gold medal, they may well have something musical to offer which other people can appreciate, admire and enjoy.

Twenty years ago, after hearing a teenager in a choir singing like a nightingale in a local Town Hall Christmas Concert, the local vicar asked why she wasn't taking up singing professionally. Her teacher invited him to have a chat with her, where he soon realised that, outside the singing world, she was a pupil with learning dificulties. Who knows what she could have achieved if she had been a teenager today – in a more inclusive setting?

I taught a pupil, once, a boy with autism. Every time he came into the music lessons he would go to the piano and play an augmented chord. It was always the same augmented chord. His uncle, who always hated the sound, would beg me to teach his nephew 'Hot Cross Buns', but the boy wouldn't play. The uncle did not understand the standard to which the pupil was actually working.

I taught another pupil, a boy with learning difficulties and poor motor skills. It was with such an effort that he moved from one note on the keyboard to the next. The day he played 'Hot Cross Buns' recognisably in time we cheered, and when his mother came to collect him, she said, 'Is that it?'

Ensembles

Ensembles (from the French for 'together') provide excellent opportunities for pupils to work together, accommodating all the various types and standards of contribution.

Many pupils with learning difficulties enjoy performing. It helps if the teacher can choose tunes that are already familiar and are rhythmically straightforward, and give careful consideration to the parts given to these students. Short pieces of music with lots of repetition in are useful and verses, lines or bars of music can be shared between pupils.

However simple the part, the teacher should rehearse it seriously with pupils so that the contribution is meaningful. Performing on stage can mean a lot to pupils with learning difficulties. They will love it. This is the day they feel really good about themselves. It takes a special place in their memory.

For those who have perfect pitch or sense of rhythm performing provides a great opportunity, and they will gain in confidence as a result of doing something that they are demonstrably good at. Pupils with Down's Syndrome are often enthusiastic singers whose performances bring pleasure to others, including families and classmates.

Most pupils with MLD/SLD will be eager to take a meaningful part in school assemblies alongside their classmates. Working together as an ensemble means that students develop a greater understanding and tolerance of difference and diversity in school. This is good for everybody – but may take some time in setting up.

Pupils with MLD like karaoke-type events and often know all the words to songs [sometimes from the unlikeliest eras]. With these pupils it is best to avoid songs with lots of complicated text and to teach them to sing 'la' when they forget the words. For solo performances or duets, choose a short piece that the pupils know very well. Always leave the audience wanting more – and not wishing there were less!

When it comes to composition the teacher should give a pupil with MLD the smallest musical idea and allow him/her to develop it further for themselves.

For pupils with BESD

Attention-seeking pupils crave two types of attention: praise/applause/recognition for their achievements and being told off for ruining something. Being the one pupil, for example, who plays the last note (after everyone else has finished,) or the one who disrupts someone else's performance, gains them much-wanted attention for not fitting in.

Performance and public performance is a time to harness and channel those needs. Pupils with BESD are often frustrated and clever and are likely to prove skilled performers; they could do well on stage provided that they don't use it as an opportunity to gain the wrong type of attention. If the pupil with BESD/ADHD starts to look as if s/he is about to kick off and spoil a performance for everyone, be firm and cut their act. If they don't turn their behaviour around this time, they will the next time.

Public performance (from classroom to stage, to the local old folks' home) is invaluable for the pupils with attention and behaviour problems. Besides all the things that performance is good for making you do, such as refining and improving your playing and giving a purpose to what may otherwise seem boring repetition, it can also make a difference to the pupils' long-term behaviour.

Such venues as old folks' homes, nurseries and hospitals are good for pupils who are very self-centred. It gives them a chance to think about others, and select and extend their repertoire accordingly – learning nursery songs for younger children, or old-time favourites for senior citizens. It can provide opportunities for them to attract the right sort of attention and earn praise for their efforts.

In the classroom it is important that pupils with BESD develop good routines. Unless the teacher is firm (and has turned all the keyboards off centrally) they will be the ones who move over to the instruments and start to play before they have listened to the instructions about what it is they have to do. (Always keep instructions as brief as possible to avoid this sort of problem.)

They may try to take the best drum-kit for themselves, or the most up-to-date keyboard etc., unless their equipment is clearly labelled and/or clear instructions are given at the start of the lesson. Prompts posted on the wall, such as 'Leave the drum-kits set up as you find them' can be useful.

It is a good idea to let the pupils with BESD have a trial set of sessions with the peripatetic teacher where they can get some more individualised tuition. However, it is sensible to send them with at least one other person, and never put the peripatetic in the position of being in a one-to-one with a pupil with behaviour problems. Recent high-profile cases serve to remind staff that they must be aware of the danger of students making false allegations against them.

For pupils with BESD, patronising and inaccurate praise will only confirm for them that adults are not serious, do not tell the truth, and can actually underestimate their pupils. It is important to be sincere at all times and develop ways of giving positive feedback even when the performance is less than brilliant; 'I can see that that was a difficult piece for you Jack, but well done for giving it a go'.

Pupils with physical difficulties

When getting pupils with cerebral palsy and other physical difficulties started at performing, the teacher should try to see what pupils can do for themselves. Playing in real time is a problem for some. Their ears will tell them what they want to hear, their eyes will tell them where to go, but their hands just won't do it.

However, there isn't much point in holding the pupil's hand in order that they can grip the beater and bang the chime, because then they are not controlling the sound. Consider getting them to operate instruments and equipment with other parts of their body, if they don't get far with their hands. They may need switches, which can make almost any sound using Soundbeam or Midi creator. (See Chapter Five on instruments and book by Margaret Corke.)

At one school which prided itself on entering pupils with all sorts of SEN for the music exam, the support assistant and the peripatetic SEN music specialist were putting together the portfolio of recordings for Anastasia, a Year 11 girl with Cerebral Palsy. Despite the extra difficulties that Anastasia has encountered, with help from the various teachers and support staff she was in with a chance of a GCSE Grade C. But, when it came to thinking about who was going to realise the composition and sing it for her, the girl begged the staff not to have her record her own song because, as she said herself, 'Even I can't tell what words I've sung'.

When putting pupils with physical difficulties on the stage the teacher must ensure that the pupils fees comfortable about their position, and that their contribution is meaningful.

At the Town Hall we once watched as a boy in a wheelchair was hoisted by two stage hands up onto the stage. Diane was thinking what would happen in a fire; Dave was thinking, 'how scary'; I was thinking, 'How undignified!'; Natalie was thinking, 'I wouldn't dream of doing that'. And the health and safety officer was thinking about the men's backs – six weeks off work looming.

Physical access to and within public spaces (wherever possible) is now a right for everyone – so plan ahead with staff at concert halls etc. to be prepared for installing moveable ramps, borrowing a hoist etc. for the performance day.

When pupils with physical difficulties go on stage, make sure they are comfortable with their position and that their contribution is meaningful.

There are some easy steps to successfully including students with physical difficulties in performance.

- Using switches – improvising over others' playing

- Operating equipment with parts of the body over which they have perfect control, e.g. feet or head

- Computers using step time

- Making atmospheric sounds not needing precise rhythms etc. [e.g. ocean drum, not wood block]

- Paired work with mainstream pupils, or pupils with complementary strengths and needs

- Wheelchair dancing

- Short extracts, limited number of notes, large instruments

- The pupil acting as composer.

Pupils with sensory impairment

In order to perform accurately pupils with hearing impairment will need good visual clues, and may also need to watch their hands while they play. These pupils will benefit from lots of rhythm work using African drums and hand-held percussion. To stay in time they can either feel the vibrations through the floor [or through a sounding board], and/or watch others for visual clues. They will respond well to graphic notation and visual directions. Singing to the Kodály hand signs will guide them towards the correct pitch. Singing into a tuner is a good way to know if you're pitching accurately.

These pupils may knock instruments out of tune and be generally unaware of dynamics. Placing grains on a drum can teach awareness of dynamics.

Pupils with hearing impairments are going to want to be up there on stage performing with the rest of their classmates, but it will be harder in general for them to stay in time and pitch with the others. Obviously, pupils with severe hearing difficulties will not hear applause. (The convention for applause in the deaf community is to wave hands in the air, not to clap – this is something that schools may like to consider if they have pupils with HI.) They will rely on their signer rather than the teacher, not looking directly at the teacher or band leader.

One type of performance practised within the deaf community is signed singing, and some deaf people (e.g. Paul Whittaker) make an art form of this by poeticising the words in order that the signing is artistic. This can be a very enjoyable and worthwhile activity for the whole class – contact the local centre for deaf people to ask if someone can come into school and teach the class a short signed song.

Performances give pupils with visual impairments the chance to shine. They are not distracted by unnecessary visuals, but they may be distracted by lesser noises that other pupils will filter out (e.g. sound of distant car horns or the central heating).

Some pupils with visual impairment may have a particular talent for music. However a pupil with visual impairment and MLD for example is going to be more than doubly disadvantaged. There are some 'savants' – disabled people who are exceptionally gifted – but they are very rare.

Visually impaired pupils will need assistance initially with finding their way around the music room and various instruments, and will need appropriate help from their support staff until they have learned where everything is and gained confidence. In the case of public performance – especially outside school – appoint a partner for the VI pupil to make sure s/he has appropriate support in unfamiliar surroundings and is kept safe. The sense of occasion will be different for pupils with visual impairment – but no less exciting; they will need to be alerted to the size of the audience, and trained to face forward and how to be part of a stage team.

Pupils with communication difficulties

Liberated from the need for conventional language pupils with Semantic Pragmatic Disorder should be more on a level with their mainstream peers during performing sessions. They may find great satisfaction from singing chunks of text.

Pupils with Asperger's Syndrome sometimes have a particular focus for music, and may be skilled at playing an instrument and relish performing. These pupils are sometimes able to compose intricate pieces of music, which can be almost impossible to play (especially if they are created on a computer). However, the pupil may be greatly distressed if even one note of his composition is played incorrectly.

A pianist in Leeds played a piece which was written by a 15-year-old boy with autism. He had envisaged it a lot faster than she played it, not realising that it made it almost impossible to play for anyone except a top class performer – or perhaps a computer. (Apparently Bartók was like this – every piece was timed to the second and had to be performed accurately.) The boy was distraught that his composition had been realised wrongly, and not exactly as he had written it.

In the classroom pupils with autism may find it difficult to accept direction from an adult. They need to develop coping routines or explore music through intensive interaction, doing paired work with their support assistant or with another pupil from the class (see Wendy Prevezer's book and articles about musical interaction). A pupil with autism who is due to perform a piece at a public concert may withdraw at the eleventh hour – make sure that you always have a substitute standing by.

All of these pupils may find the idea of being watched by an audience very disturbing. They should not be offered for performance unless their teachers, support staff and parents/carers feel confident that this is a good idea. Even so, there should be an escape route planned.

The school concert

Here is the dilemma. The concert is where the public sees the school, where prospective parents can compare high schools, where the rest of the school views what the music department has been doing. The concert should be where the pupils present what they can do, what they have learnt and what they have practised.

Should you audition? If so, what would be your criteria for letting people up on stage, and should you set different rules for pupils with SEN?

The concert at the outside venue

Once you have decided to take pupils with special needs to the Town Hall or the local residential care home, you have to

- consider the risks

- fill in a risk assessment

There is a danger with risk assessment forms that, once you have filled in the form you feel that you have somehow lessened the risk. Thinking seriously about the pitfalls that trips present is helpful. The teacher may have to conclude that some risks are too high.

Special events for special needs

There are occasions where pupils and adults with special needs get together musically and exclusively. Pupils and their carers, parents and support workers appreciate these events where all the musical activities are geared towards those with SEN, and they all can compare notes. In the north of England there is YAMSEN (see Appendix 1 for information) and the Wharfedale Festival which has a category for entrants with SEN, and others.

Composing and improvising

When a pupil is comfortable with their chosen medium (i.e. instrument) composition is a good place to explore and organise their thoughts and ideas outside the rules of the speaking/writing world, through another language or means of communication that is music.

Improvising is good because there are no rules. The teacher can set as few or as many boundaries as s/he wants. Pupils are liberated from the fear of playing the 'wrong' note, because there are no wrong notes, no wrong rhythms, no wrong combinations of instruments, no wrong switches. By listening to what they achieve accidentally pupils will learn about their instruments and themselves musically, and then repeat anything that pleases them.

Obviously this is the same for mainstream pupils but improvising is liberating for pupils who have less control over their movements, or for those who can't easily play recognisable songs. It is also good for pupils who don't communicate in the conventional way.

Summing up performance

Your inclusive performance suite/room will contain many extras in order to include all the pupils with all their different special needs. While this requires quite a considerable reorganisation in the first place, it will result in benefiting all the pupils, as of course inclusion is intended to do. The able bodied will enjoy the switches. The pupils with BESD will have to work in pairs or groups. This is an opportunity for pupils to work together.

However, you will need to be on top of things all the time, and you must insist on technical support, exactly when you need it. Be aware that the lesson can be ruined for a child with cerebral palsy should a pupil with behavioural difficulties pull out a wire at a crucial moment, maybe when the teacher is involved with another pupil. Support in the form of teaching assistants and/or carefully planned pairing of pupils to work together will enable the teacher to manage the whole group effectively.

Inclusion does not mean ironing out differences or getting everybody to be able to do the same thing. In music lessons, if there are 21 pupils in a classroom, there may be 21 different activities going on simultaneously. Inclusive music lessons highlight and celebrate differences rather than endure them.

CHAPTER 7

Listening

Music is everywhere. It provides a background to doing homework and housework, it is in our cars, in the supermarket, department stores, pubs and restaurants. With personal stereo systems, we listen to music sitting on buses and trains and walking down the street. We dance to it, in our wheelchairs and on our feet. We walk down the aisle to it, bury our loved ones to it; Prokofiev announces the arrival of Newcastle United, and Gerry and the Pacemakers bring on Liverpool.

The makers of films, television programmes, radio programmes and advertisements use music, newly composed or already existing, to announce beginnings and endings, and to set scenes and moods.

Music that someone else has composed and recorded forms a big part of our culture and everyday experience. Pupils will form their friendships around a particular style of 'pop' music and their musical tastes around their friendships, but though they may listen to 'chart' music as played on radio, they will also hear snippets of classical music on TV and radio advertisements and at football grounds, and may even have to endure Classic FM or Radio 3 while being taxied round by their parents.

> One teacher decided to introduce some new songs from a particular style of music to her pupils. She played Tammy Wynnette. 'I know that,' said Simon, 'That's *Stand by your man*'. 'That's right,' said the teacher, as she pressed PLAY for Kenny Rogers. '*Lucille*,' Simon sang along with the lyrics. 'Well, Simon,' the teacher smiled, 'and who is this?' 'Dolly Parton, *DIVORCE*' was the correct reply.
>
> It turned out that the bus driver was a country and western fan, and that for the past six months Simon had a veritable history of music lesson as he was transported to and from school every day.

But most of the time, music is played as a background to other activities, so it should come as little surprise that *Listening* is one of the hardest components of the music course. Teachers are asking pupils to listen out for instruments that they rarely, if ever, hear or see, and to have an emotional response to classical music that may be well outside their normal experience. And they are being asked to be quiet for a sustained period. Teaching pupils to listen critically, and with discernment is a challenging part of the music curriculum.

Pupils with learning and behavioural difficulties

Above all other components of the music curriculum, listening for pupils with BESD is possibly the hardest. Some pupils find it difficult to put aside their other thoughts and their problems, and lose themselves in listening to this other language that is music. (It's easy to overlook the fact that pupils bring all sorts of baggage into the classroom – the aftermath of a row at home, concerns about money worries about a drug-taking sibling. Taking time to learn something about pupils, even if you see them only once a week, is always worth doing.)

Pupils will come into the room with all sorts of other things in their head. Concentration may be better in the morning than in the afternoon when they are getting tired. Alternatively, some classes are very sluggish first period. Some pupils may find it difficult to settle down on Monday mornings after the week-end. Sometimes they are on a high after a particular lesson such as drama.

In teaching students to listen to and appreciate music, it is essential to plan the order in which you play musical excerpts to a class. Starting with a calm piece can help to settle a 'lively' group.

The aim will be to get the whole class listening and thinking in silence, but this may have to be reached in gradual stages, with modest expectations – and short pieces of music to start with. The list of suggestions below may be helpful:

- be aware that some pupils will need to be actively taught how to listen well (see chart on following page)

- some simple relaxation exercises can help pupils to be calm

- encourage the use of 'stress reducers' to counteract fidgeting

- select familiar pieces of music at first (for classical, world etc.) and keep sequences fairly short

- repeat the same lesson format every time to establish a routine

- have some question sheets (e.g. Foxwood Listening Scheme) to focus their attention; include open as well as closed questions

- have key words strategically placed around the room and/or on the tables

- use visual as well as audio input (e.g. videos, interactive whiteboard software)

- reward good listening by playing a song from the charts for the last piece of music or at the end of the lesson

- use the school's behaviour management system consistently and fairly

If question sheets are to be used they will need to be differentiated in order to accommodate reading and writing difficulties.

Many pupils find reading difficult for a whole variety of reasons. The majority of texts are still black print on a white background and this is uncomfortable for some categories of readers. Pupils with dyslexia may use a coloured plastic overlay to obviate the problem of 'glare'. However, they still may find it harder to write on white paper. Schools could ease this problem by making paper available in a range of colours. (See following page for advice on producing classroom materials.)

Listening is a skill

Sit comfortably.

Relax – let your shoulders drop, close your eyes, breathe in deeply to the count of three/four; hold the breath for three/four; breathe out for three/four. Repeat this a few times.

Think about what you are listening for – particular instruments, pace, technique?

Keep still while you are listening.

Do not speak until the teacher asks you to.

Producing your own materials

Here are some guidelines for creating listening/question sheets.

Fonts	Arial, Universe and New Century Schoolbook are easier to read than other fonts.
Font size	12 or 14 is best for most pupils
Font format	**Bold** is OK; *italic* is hard to read
Layout	Use lots of headings and subheadings as signposts, leave lots of space between lines and paragraphs.
CAPITAL LETTERS	These are hard to read so use sparingly.
Consistency	Ensure instructions and symbols are used consistently
Provide answers	If pupils can check answers (to closed questions) for themselves, they learn more and become more independent.
Enlarging	It is better to enlarge text by using a bigger font on a word processor rather than relying on the photocopier. Photocopied enlargements can appear fuzzy and A3 paper never fits neatly in exercise books or folders.
Forms	If you are making an answer sheet or cloze exercise, remember that partially sighted pupils often have handwriting that is larger than average, so allow extra space on forms. This will also help pupils with learning difficulties who have immature or poorly formed writing or are still printing.
Spacing	Keep to the same amount of space between each word. Do not use justified text as the uneven word spacing can make reading more difficult
Alignment	Align text to the left margin. This makes it easier to find the start and finish of each line. It ensures an even space between each word.
Placing illustrations	Do not wrap text around images if it means that lines of text will start in different places. Do not have text going over images as this makes it hard to read.

Pupils with physical difficulties

A pupil whose ability to go anywhere depends on other people may well have spent much time listening to music. If they have had little access to switches, which enable them to control their environment, they may have listened to other people's music and developed specific tastes, which are different from their peers.

The pupil could build up a listening, concert, and musical activities profile. This will be a good guide to their interest and abilities and can be used as a starting point for them to move off from. Listening in class should develop social awareness of other people's tastes.

There are very few adjustments needed in the Listening session for pupils with physical difficulties. The most severely disabled won't need to write. Some may make notes on their laptops. After the playing has finished they may need a discussion with their TA about what they have just heard. The teacher must establish that the pupil and support worker should not talk during the musical excerpts. Also, the TA will establish whether the person in a wheelchair is comfortable enough to sit quite still for the duration.

Pupils with sensory impairment

A British sign language teacher was discussing the education of Deaf and Hearing Impaired pupils with a high school music teacher
'Do you teach music to the deaf' he signed.
'Of course' she signed. 'I wouldn't want anyone excluded from my lessons.'
'What's the point?' he shrugged and signed.

Even with 95 per cent hearing loss, the pupils with hearing impairment will get a lot of pleasure from listening. These pupils need to be near the speakers, on a resonant floor and/or with their own amplifier-receivers. Having videos of orchestras and bands may help, although the totally deaf may get nothing from them. Live acoustic instrumental music can be more accessible for these pupils than CDs. Visual displays on an interactive white board with computer generated patterns can help.

The teacher may invite pupils to clap along with some pieces of music. In that case, the pupils with HI will enjoy the social interaction of clapping along with them. Do not be afraid to ask whether or not they can hear and what they can hear. For the totally deaf the benefits of a listening lesson are debatable.

Pupils who are blind or VI live in a world of sound. They may enjoy a large and varied listening repertoire at an early age. Like the pupils with physical difficulties they may have a wide varied eclectic and eccentric repertoire. The teacher must be sensitive to their extra knowledge. Listening will increase their understanding of the music that they already know.

The teacher must just ensure that there are no extraneous noises which would distract the blind pupils but which normally don't bother other people. These could be the noise of the central heating or the buzz of a poorly recorded piece of music.

To make notes the blind pupils will have Braille and/or Screenwriter, and those with VI may prefer extra-large print.

Pupils with communication difficulties

Sitting in a group of other people who are being quiet, listening and concentrating on the music will benefit the pupils on the autistic spectrum. It is good for them as a social activity. For a few of them it will be a marvellous voyage of discovery as they finally find the type of music that they really adore. Pupils with autism may find it hard to sit for any length of time, but, being selective, may really enjoy listening to a long piece of music.

Staff must allow for these pupils' tastes. They can be obsessive about certain pieces and may need steering away from some pieces. Listening should be a calming experience, but the teacher needs to rely on the TA to assess how the session is going and to have an alternative activity.

Of all the music course's components, listening probably needs adjusting the least in order to accommodate pupils with SEN. Make music a multi-sensory experience. Allow pupils to move materials and scarves in time with the music and link the emotions expressed in the music to textures such as sand paper and velvet to define the different types of sounds.

Of course, for most people there is nothing like a live concert, for those with or without SEN. This is a truly multi-sensory experience as pupils see, hear and feel music.

If you're doing listening properly you are reaching into the students' own world, touching their own culture and leaving the comfort of your own knowledge and tastes behind. You will also of course be asking them to enter into the unfamiliar worlds of music they may have never heard before. You may be opening doors for pupils to whom so many doors are closed.

CHAPTER 8

Monitoring and Assessment

Generally, assessment in music can buzz along at the discretion and judgement of the music staff, until it comes to reports and then everybody wants a 'level'. Pupils don't ask anymore, 'Did I play that song well?' They ask, 'Why did you give Shanelle a 4a and me only a 3b?'

Monitoring and assessing pupils can be motivating for the pupils themselves, to help them see what they have achieved and what else they could do. However, just allocating numbers isn't going to steer pupils towards their musical future. It would be far better to identify what skills and what knowledge that each pupil has developed and get the pupil to note these on their own record sheets (see CD for suggested record sheets). This is more important for pupils with SEN, for whom the numbers may seem like a reminder of failure.

If teachers use the indexes and lesson content cover sheets as suggested on the CD, the pupils will build up a tangible list of subjects and skills covered, and in a non-competitive and unthreatening way. In this way all pupils with SEN can easily be included. Using boxes for notes or for the name of songs learnt etc. is a more dynamic and exciting way of recording achievement than having a bank of sentences beginning 'I can . . .'

Most music teachers already keep sets of tape recordings (easier now on computers) for individual pupils and individual classes, and can demonstrate progress by reminding pupils what they sounded like last year compared to what they can do now. Blind pupils and those with VI will appreciate this method of measuring progress, and they will probably be better than others at noting the progress in depth.

Pupils with SEN should have an IEP (individual education plan) or IBP (Individual behaviour plan) (examples on the CD), which will identify the pupil's educational needs that are additional to and different from those accommodated in a differentiated lesson. When it comes to playing and using musical instruments and equipment the music teacher may need to add some targets of her/his own. It may be that a pupil will also come with a musical gift, and this should also be recognised and the students' specific needs met.

The National Curriculum levels can be interpreted to suit all sorts of pupils, but for those with significant learning difficulties, there are P levels.

The P levels are intended as a form of teacher assessment for children working significantly below age-related expectations, who are unlikely to achieve beyond level 2 by the time they leave secondary school.

Systems for providing training and moderation in using the P scales are developing in many LEAs, and are likely to become more widespread in future. You may be able to access support from your LEA, or from a local special school where staff have experience in using the scales. *B Squared* assessment files are a popular way of recording small steps of achievement and the music file will be available from Autumn 2005 (www.bsquaredsen.co.uk).

Performance descriptions across subjects

The performance descriptions for P1 to P3 are common across all subjects. They outline the types and range of general performance that pupils with learning difficulties might characteristically demonstrate. Subject-focused examples are included to illustrate some of the ways in which staff might identify attainment in different subject contexts.

P1 (i) Pupils encounter activities and experiences. They may be passive or resistant. They may show simple reflex responses, *for example, startling at sudden noises or movements.* Any participation is fully prompted.

P1 (ii) Pupils show emerging awareness of activities and experiences. They may have periods when they appear alert and ready to focus their attention on certain people, events, objects or parts of objects, *for example, becoming still in a concert hall. They may give intermittent reactions, for example, sometimes becoming excited at repeated patterns of sounds.*

P2 (i) Pupils begin to respond consistently to familiar people, events and objects. They react to new activities and experiences, for example, turning towards unfamiliar sounds. They begin to show interest in people, events and objects, for example, looking for the source of music. They accept and engage in coactive exploration, *for example, being encouraged to stroke the strings of a guitar.*

P2 (ii) Pupils begin to be proactive in their interactions. They communicate consistent preferences and affective responses, for example, relaxing during certain pieces of music but not others. They recognise familiar people, events and objects, *for example, a favourite song.* They perform actions, often by trial and improvement, and they remember learned responses over short periods of time, *for example, repeatedly pressing the keys of an electronic keyboard instrument.* They co-operate with shared exploration and supported participation, *for example, holding an ocean drum.*

P3 (i) Pupils begin to communicate intentionally. They seek attention through eye contact, gesture or action. They request events or activities, *for example, leading an adult to the CD player.* They participate in shared activities with less support. They sustain concentration for short periods. They explore materials in increasingly complex ways, *for example, tapping piano keys gently and with more vigour.* They observe the results of their own actions with interest, *for example, listening intently when moving across and through a sound beam.* They remember learned responses over more extended periods, *for example, recalling movements associated with a particular song from week to week.*

P3 (ii) Pupils use emerging conventional communication. They greet known people and may initiate interactions and activities, *for example, performing an action such as clapping hands to initiate a particular song.* They can remember learned responses over increasing periods of time and may anticipate known events, for example, a loud sound at a particular point in a piece of music. They may respond to options and choices with actions or gestures, *for example, choosing a shaker in a rhythm band activity.* They actively explore objects and events for more extended periods, *for example, tapping, stroking, rubbing or shaking an instrument to produce various effects.* They apply potential solutions systematically to problems, *for example, indicating by eye contact or gesture the pupil whose turn it is to play in a 'call and response' activity.*

Performance descriptions in music

From levels P4 to P8, many believe it is possible to describe pupils' performance in a way that indicates the emergence of skills, knowledge and understanding in music. The descriptions provide an example of how this can be done.

P4 Pupils use single words, gestures, signs, objects, pictures or symbols to communicate about familiar musical activities or name familiar instruments. With some support, they listen and attend to familiar musical activities and follow and join in familiar routines. They are aware of cause and effect in familiar events, *for example, what happens when particular instruments are shaken, banged, scraped or blown, or that a sound can be started and stopped or linked to movement through a sound beam.* They begin to look for an instrument or noisemaker played out of sight. They repeat, copy and imitate actions, sounds or words in songs and musical performances.

P5 Pupils take part in simple musical performances. They respond to signs given by a musical conductor, *for example, to start or stop playing.* They pick out a specific musical instrument when asked, *for example, a drum or a triangle.* They play loudly, quietly, quickly and slowly in imitation. They play an instrument when prompted by a cue card. They listen to, and imitate, distinctive sounds played on a particular instrument. They listen to a familiar instrument played behind a screen and match the sound to the correct instrument on a table.

P6 Pupils respond to other pupils in music sessions. They join in and take turns in songs and play instruments with others. They begin to play, sing and move expressively in response to the music or the meaning of words in a song. They explore the range of effects that can be made by an instrument or sound maker. They copy simple rhythms and musical patterns or phrases. They can play groups of sounds indicated by a simple picture or symbol-based score. They begin to categorise percussion instruments by how they can be played, *for example, striking or shaking.*

P7 Pupils listen to music and can describe music in simple terms, *for example, describing musical experiences using phrases or statements combining a small number of words, signs, symbols or gestures.* They respond to prompts to play faster, slower, louder, softer. They follow simple graphic scores with symbols or pictures and play simple patterns or sequences of music. Pupils listen and contribute to sound stories, are involved in simple improvisation and make basic choices about the sound and instruments used. They make simple compositions, *for example, by choosing symbols or picture cue cards, ordering them from left to right, or making patterns of sounds using computer software.*

P8 Pupils listen carefully to music. They understand and respond to words, symbols and signs that relate to tempo, dynamics and pitch, *for example, faster, slower, louder, higher, and lower.* They create their own simple compositions, carefully selecting sounds. They create simple graphic scores using pictures or symbols. They use a growing musical vocabulary of words, signs or symbols to describe what they play and hear, *for example, fast, slow, high, low.* They make and communicate choices when performing, playing, composing, listening and appraising, *for example, prompting members of the group to play alone, in partnerships, in groups or all together.*

Pupils with learning and behavioural difficulties

Pupils with emotional problems may have no additional learning difficulty, but their reading and writing skills may be less well developed than their other academic abilities. When they are being assessed or examined it would be a good idea to have a support assistant with them in order to explain any written questions so that nothing holds back their natural musical talent from shining through and being recognised.

Pupils with PMLD, SLD, MLD

It is very difficult to measure the small steps of progress made by some pupils with significant learning difficulties and record how much a pupil understands of their musical experiences. The P levels (broken down further in some parts of the country even further into PIVATS : Lancashire County Council 2002) can help and provide a way of reporting achievements that is much more positive than the old-style 'Working towards Level One' (see accompanying CD).

Pupils with MLD generally operate between levels 1 and 3 at high school, and, in exceptional cases, with a lot of support, could be entered for GCSE Music. However, there are alternative accreditations from the Welsh Exam Board (see Appendix 1).

Pupils with dyslexia and dyscalculia

These pupils' special educational needs should not affect their ability to play or to listen with understanding. All the Expressive Arts subjects give these pupils a chance to achieve equally with their fellow pupils. You may have to do some writing in music lessons, but this is only as a means to a practical end. You should be careful about assessing written work, and, if the dyslexia is severe, you should be able to give extra time for writing or hire an amanuensis for examinations.

Pupils with dyspraxia have motor skills problems and tend to be clumsy. Teachers will need to assess pupils' fine motor skills in order to offer access to the most appropriate instruments and activities.

Pupils with physical difficulties

The difficulty here is that what the pupil can hear inside their head is not what they are able to reproduce with their body, and they may have problems with performance. In order to assess and compare these pupils fairly, the teacher and the TA should allow longer for the tests, put in the notes etc. to be played in real time, and then use the programme to realise their intentions. (Most sequencing programmes have a step-time input.) If the end result is a low grade, then be honest.

Pupils with sensory impairment

Somebody who is profoundly deaf is unlikely to be as successful as their peers in the usual school music activities. Teachers shouldn't feel pressurised into giving a level or grade for the sake of it, nor grades above the pupils' actual ability. It may be appropriate to declare n/a (not appropriate) on some parts of the assessment forms and reports.

However, there are notable exceptions to this general rule. If a deaf pupil wants to go along the exam route, then the teacher should contact Music for the Deaf (see Appendix 1).

Although blind and visually-impaired pupils will exhibit the usual full range of musical abilities, teachers may expect them to be disproportionately successful in music. Sight-reading forms a very small part of music exams, and can be replaced by aural tests. It is possible for pupils familiar with Braille music to be tested on it.

For assessing pupils for GCSEs and A levels it is recommended that teachers approach the RNIB directly, and speak to the education officer.

Pupils with communication difficulties

Probably the hardest thing about assessing pupils on the ASD spectrum is catching them demonstrating their abilities or their successes. There is no reason not to use the normal NC levels for these pupils, though these may not truly reflect a child's ability in music. Very occasionally, a teacher may come across a child with ASD who has a particular gift for music – to the point of being a 'genius' in that one area of ability. Teachers need to nurture such gifts and allow them to flourish.

For most pupils with SEN, being measured against their peers is only ever going to amount to failing. Teachers should investigate and devise parallel methods of assessment and recording in order to avoid demotivating pupils in their classes who get high marks for effort on reports, but low marks for achievement.

A teacher wanting to monitor the progress of the pupils with SEN could look to the snapshot systems already in use. One is the traffic lights system (quickly noting red, orange or green in the mark book); another is jotting down +, = or –, according to whether they are reaching their targets.

Target setting and tracking a pupil's progress is already commonplace. It is a good way of looking out for pupils who are underachieving and gives the school's pastoral heads a chance to investigate for problems outside school.

As pupils with SEN progress through school, any aptitude for music is unlikely to be reflected in other subjects, so effective tracking may throw up some interesting anomalies which would suggest that the very musical pupil with SEN should be directed towards more musical activities (college course, extra lessons, local youth groups, even more lessons in school time).

Teachers are already aware of the dangers of grading, and the artificial and superficial conclusions that may be drawn from it. When schools have Awards Evenings they generally present in-house certificates for performing at the Civic Hall or the local primary school, or contributing to the life of the school. They may also have certificates from their local Music Support Service for musical development days and concert tours.

Monitoring and assessment should be there to serve the pupil. IEPs which are drawn up to tell staff what a pupil's difficulties and needs are could also have a statement identifying their musical strengths (and how they will contribute to the pupil's social and learning development).

CHAPTER 9

Working with Teaching Assistants

Additional in-class support can be provided for pupils with SEN by parent volunteers, support service teachers or teaching assistants. These assistants come in many shapes and forms, from dinner staff improving their occupational skills to psychology graduates. Essentially their presence in the classroom should enable you to teach the whole class and its individuals better than if they were not there.

The aim of such support is for the TA to use a range of intervention and support strategies during each lesson in order to:

- Facilitate maximum participation in and access to the curriculum for pupils with SEN

- Encourage pupils to remain focused and on task

- Reduce the incidence of disruptive behaviour

- Foster greater pupil independence

- Increase pupils' confidence and self-esteem

- Raise attainment

Whatever the TA's educational training and experience, the Arts, especially the music lesson, presents certain challenges. Many support staff will come from the time when music was regarded as a talent, not a school subject available to all. Their childhood experience can have been traumatic, and whole industries have grown up around the fact that so many people were told in their youth that they could not sing.

In general, what is so sad and so frustrating is that teaching assistants often preface their presence in your classroom with the opinion that they are 'not musical'. Do they venture into Humanities, I wonder, with the words, 'I am not geographical'?

Whatever their level of confidence, TAs will appreciate guidance from the teacher about their role in the music lesson and the ways in which they can support pupils. The following list may help to negotiate an agreement:

The role of the TA in music lessons

- Clarifying and explaining instructions, questions, tasks

- Keeping pupils on task

- Overseeing the setting up and care of instruments and equipment

- Assisting with recording (written, audio, video)

- Reading or helping pupils to read written material

- Assisting pupils in instrument practice

- Monitoring pupil behaviour

- Differentiating tasks and materials

- Encouraging and praising pupils

- Helping pupils to work towards their IEP targets

- Keeping teachers informed of difficulties encountered by pupils

- Suggesting to the teacher ways in which pupils could access the music curriculum more easily

- Providing basic writing equipment for pupils; encouraging pupils to participate in ensemble work and group/class discussion

- Developing positive relationships with pupils

- Contributing information about pupils' progress

Support staff are increasingly financed by the statements for individual pupils with MLD or EBD, but it is not always judged the best use of their time to be with these pupils all day. As inclusion becomes a reality in our schools, however, some support staff may be 'permanently attached' to their charges. The classroom teacher needs to be aware of these situations and plan how to manage the time in music lessons – for both the student and the TA. It may be the case that the TA finds herself 'taking over' from the pupil – answering questions for him, setting up instruments, even playing them, rather than always encouraging the student to be as independent as possible.

Alternatively, the TA may feel that she knows nothing about music and can therefore 'take a backseat in these lessons' – that she has nothing to offer.

A peripatetic teacher was introducing steel pans to a class in a particularly difficult but musical inner-city school. Two women were sitting chatting at the back of the room while the teacher set up all the instruments, chose which pupils would partner each other, and started teaching. The class teacher (who had the other half of the class next door) called in to see how things were going. The peripatetic teacher asked who the women were, because their chat was a bit distracting. 'Oh, they're support assistants' she said, somewhat wearily.

One area where music differs from other subjects is in the need, at times, for total silence. This can be when pupils are asked to respond emotionally to a piece of music, recorded or live. There is a danger that TAs may regard their charges and themselves exempt from this silence. The TA may even feel that she is 'not earning her money' if she merely sits and listens to music. It is important for the teacher to discuss these issues with TAs and to establish, from the outset, a mutually beneficial way of working.

The list below provides some suggested ways in which teachers can support their TAs and maximise their input:

- Be clear about your expectations – read their job descriptions and talk to them about how their role might develop in music lessons

- Think about the TA's role when planning lessons

- Inform the TA in advance about what the aims of the lesson will be and the tasks involved

- Make opportunities for joint planning and sharing of ideas (it doesn't have to be an after-school 'meeting' – it can be over a sandwich at lunch or an informal chat over coffee)

- Ask the TA for ideas on how to differentiate for particular pupils

- Encourage the TA to use their own initiative and demonstrate any musical talent, taking care, by doing so, that they don't engender any feeling of inadequacy in the pupils

- Establish clear procedures for discipline in the lesson

- Share feedback on the lesson and on individual pupil's achievements

- Acknowledge the TA when talking to pupils – the better their status with them, the more effective they can be

- Remember to show your appreciation; be prepared to praise when things go well, and to share responsibility when they don't

Teaching assistants and the pupils with learning and behavioural difficulties

For pupils with MLD and SLD

These pupils can be the most difficult pupils to assess when you first meet them. In appearance, they may look like the rest of the class. The teacher's only clue to the fact that they have a difficulty may indeed be the presence of the assistant.

The support assistant will translate the lesson for the pupil, extracting what they can do, and helping them achieve. The music teacher must look to these TAs to advise them on how much or how little the pupils with SLD can manage. Pupils with MLD often arrive without a support assistant, but they would probably benefit from some extra personal attention.

Pupils with PMLD are likely to be supported by experienced teaching assistants who know the pupil well and teachers should draw on this knowledge when planning appropriate activities for music lessons.

Pupils with BESD

Some TAs are behaviour management specialists. Some are not. With the right training behaviour support workers can keep the pupil with behaviour problems on task and in the classroom. Unfortunately, it is common for the behaviour support worker to be a different person in every lesson. Thus the pupil with EBD does not get the chance to build up a relationship with a significant adult.

The TA for a pupil with BESD needs a pocket full of stationery, a dictionary full of avoidance tactics and infinite patience. They must take care not to overrule or undermine the teacher in matters of discipline and be ready to remove the pupil from the room with minimum disruption to the lesson.

Teaching assistants and the pupils with physical difficulties

Every Friday morning for half a term the support assistant would wheel William into his music lesson. Both William and the assistant loved this lesson and the teacher loved having them there. William was especially fond of improvising. He and his support assistant did this with the Alesis's AirFX, a DJ-ing gadget which you operate partly through a sound beam. One day just after half term William's support assistant was suddenly called out of the lesson and asked the music teacher to work with William on his own. This was when the music teacher came to realise that the support assistant had really enjoyed using the AirFX and William was desperate to have a go on the violin.

Pupils with physical difficulties can be divided into three main categories as far as how much support they need from their teaching assistants. There are those with very limited movement who rely upon switches to connect with all of the outside world. Their support staff will be with them throughout their school day, and deal with all their intimate requirements. Their support assistant will literally be 'their right hand person', and will connect them with other people.

The good thing about these support assistants is that they are very close to the pupil, and will not be afraid to tell them off, but they may also be over protective. The music teacher should introduce new ideas gently, including the support assistant as they go and, hopefully, winning them over. If any writing is required from these pupils the support assistant will act as amanuensis and will be expert at understanding the pupil's means of communicating.

Some of these pupils will have communication devices attached to their wheelchairs. These are effectively the child's voice and so the pupil must always control their use – just as a teacher would not cover a student's mouth to stop him speaking, so a communication device must not be switched off by a teacher or TA. If the use of communication aids is a concern, the teacher can ask for advice from the speech and language therapist .

The best assistants for pupils are those who allow them choice whenever possible. They will for example hold up two alternatives and ask the pupil to eye point their choice.

The support assistant, through their line manager, will be in constant communication with the parents and will be able to report back any successes identified by the teacher.

Secondly there are the pupils with such conditions as muscular dystrophy (probably with electric wheelchairs), able to use their arms but in a limited way. They need support staff to set up and position equipment, but not to operate the equipment on the pupils' behalf. Thirdly there are those who have full control of the top half of their body. They will get themselves where they need to be with little help, as long as the room is set up correctly. These are the wheelchair users who will require no extra support for your lesson. This will be obvious when you meet them.

Teaching assistants and the pupils with sensory impairment

For pupils who are hearing impaired

If your pupil who is deaf or hearing impaired comes with a signer, the pupil will watch the signer not you. Your relationship with the signer is important. If you want the pupil to take part in a singing lesson, you should give the signer the song's text well in advance so that s/he can rehearse it before the lesson. The signer may be willing to coach the pupil for a signed performance.

For pupils who are blind and visually impaired

The TA needs only to set up the environment so that the pupil can find things easily. They might act as an amanuensis. They could make sure that the music room is labelled, where appropriate, with Braille or Moon signs.

Teaching assistants and the pupils with communication difficulties

For pupils with autism

These assistants have possibly the hardest job of all of them, and possibly the most fun. To be effective in the music lesson they will need a working knowledge of musical interaction – (see Appendix 1: Wendy Prevezer) As it is likely that they will spend the whole day with the pupil they will be familiar with their obsessions and will probably already have their own methods for getting pupils to complete tasks. Some pupils with ASD can become very anxious and may run out of the room on occasions. If this is a regular occurrence, give a TA the responsibility for following the pupil, and give the child a 'get out of jail' card that can be taken to the school office or to the 'safe haven'.

Summary

It can be hard for a music teacher to manage other adults in the classroom, but mutual respect and a desire to do the best for pupils in need of support will go a long way to establishing a good working relationship. Setting aside some time for planning will pay dividends – although time is always in short supply. It can be helpful for music teachers to imagine that they have been tasked with supporting a pupil during a lesson in Russian, or higher maths – or whatever subject they are unfamiliar with. How would they go about it? Knowing the pupil and his particular needs will help, but having some knowledge of the lesson content and the teacher's objectives will be a great asset. For some pupils, just preparing them for what is going to happen in a lesson – introducing the ideas and explaining the order of activities – can make all the difference; a simple idea, but difficult for the TA to execute if she has no prior knowledge herself.

CHAPTER 10

General Principles for SEN Provision in Music

Including pupils with SEN in your music lessons will be very rewarding, but it will also be a challenge. It will require teachers to consider some physical reorganisation of the music suite and consideration of how the music curriculum can be made accessible to all.

Including pupils with BESD can be particularly challenging, and teachers and TAs should ensure that they have good preparation and training alongside a good school behaviour policy.

It may be simplistic to think of pupils with SEN as if divided into those who can't, and those that won't, but it can help to be aware that managing these different groups requires quite different skills and knowledge. Of course, there are pupils who belong to both groups – those with physical difficulties, for example, who know what they want but are unable to do it, and so become frustrated and angry. Consequently they then present the emotional and behavioural difficulties of the other group.

> Rosanna was in top set for everything, and in the GCSE Music class. She loved classical music, especially Chopin, or any piano pieces, and loved to watch music videos. Faced with having to write a piece of music for a ceremonial event, but unable to play one note after another in real time, she put her electric wheelchair into reverse, and rammed into the guitarists tuning up at the other side of the room.

Pupils with behavioural social development needs including Attention Deficit Disorder (with or without hyperactivity)

ADD/ADHD

For these pupils music may be an important but narrow cultural experience. They tend to like the latest songs in the charts, and go for heroes who are controversial and who appear to espouse violence or antagonism towards some other sub-group such as women or gays. And when they like classical, they like it loud!

Wanting to encourage her charges to like classical music, the teacher routinely played the last part of the *'William Tell Overture'* as part of her listening course. And routinely, a small group of boys used to turn round on their chairs, in effect saddle up, and 'gallop' across the room.

In the beginning of things it seems quite easy – the old three chord trick, the twelve bar blues, varying the rhythms – it's easy. Then ask them to play the bass lines, and it's not so easy. These pupils want it *now*! They do not want to stop and think about it. The Foxwood Songsheets (see Appendix 1) were designed with including these pupils in mind. Colour-coding the chords is also an excellent idea so that the better behaved can move on, while pupils with EBD can keep up.

The music lesson can be a lifeline for pupils with EBD, if they can survive the first five minutes of the lesson. They learn about sharing and co-operating. Achieving an ensemble sound is very satisfying. They can pour out all their feelings in songs, either by singing others' songs or composing their own. And since the 1960s it has become traditional to write songs about serious social and personal issues. Songwriters' lyrics and teenagers' interests have moved on from 'Saturday Night at the Movies' to 'War, what is it Good For?' It gives all students a place to think about things that hurt and confuse them, as, of course, do English, drama and art. And, like all the arts, music gives them another language of expression.

Pupils with BESD may have no additional learning difficulties and if the teacher and TAs can just get the relationship right the music rooms might become a haven for them, and performance may even be a career move. Even when pupils have no particular musical talent, they may enjoy and be calmed by successful music lessons.

Students with EBD like attention. The stage, and in public, is a good place for it. Consequently music is a popular subject, but the reality of all the components of the music course that don't require being watched can prove disappointing, and hard to handle e.g. listening, history, theory, and rehearsals.

Good behaviour management courses will give teachers a range of strategies that they can use in the classroom. (Mick Pitchford's 'Praise, Ignore, Reward' is excellent – see Appendix 1). Carfeul planning to match activities to pupils' abilities is the key to successful teaching in inclusive classrooms – you can't 'wing it'.

It must be said, you probably also need to be a special kind of teacher to be successful with

Lionel just never felt the need to sit down.

pupils who are 'hard to teach': patient, firm, flexible, strict, humorous, low-voiced, refusing to be sidetracked, capable of multitasking and, of course, passionate about teaching music.

Tourette's Syndrome

There is no reason why the pupil with Tourette's shouldn't succeed at music. It has even been suggested that Mozart had Tourette's Syndrome. The obvious problem is being quiet in a listening session. Singing may help them. If the class is used to the pupil they will have learned to ignore his (rarely her) strange sounds, and it won't irritate them as it will the teacher who sees them only once a week. Be on the look out for 'troublemakers' trying to wind up these pupils. Once they become anxious their tics become worse.

Pupils with MLD, Down's Syndrome and Fragile X Syndrome

These pupils benefit from a lesson which has the same structure every time. For example the same opening warm up and cool down for a whole half term. They can follow and enjoy simplified musical tasks and enjoy singing provided the words are not too complex. It is best to use songs with choruses, asking individuals to sing the verses. Singing 'La' to sections they can't do enables them to join in all the time with the rest of the class.

These pupils may be able to create simple compositions and be entered for Entry Level Certificate (see Appendix) which is designed to increase pupils' self-esteem.

For all pupils basic foundation activities exploring rhythm and pitch are essential. Time spent on these is usually fun and never wasted, even on the brightest of pupils. When a complex idea is introduced to pupils that have these foundations they should be able to move on at speed. The presence of pupils in the class who have learning difficulties makes any music teacher rethink their approach to standard musical tasks, usually to the benefit of the rest of the group.

The Kodály, Dalcroze and Orff teaching methods are going to produce good results. They break down the elements of music to their most basic, and use patterns of body movements, words and hand signs to imprint these ideas into the long-term memory of the pupil. With this information stored within her/his body the pupil can always move on.

Pupils with SLD and PMLD

These pupils usually like music. They often know lots of songs and pieces of music which they have picked up from their family, television and radio. Try to incorporate some of these songs into lessons to help pupils feel included and achieve success. Don't worry about playing loud music with these pupils in the room, they will probably love it.

These pupils need a multi-sensory approach where possible. This involves using lighting, fragrances, tastes, temperature, atmosphere, vibro-tactile instruments (see appendix 1), coloured materials, pictures, puppets etc. When playing untuned percussion instruments they need clear directions for stopping and starting. This may be their biggest achievement. When playing tuned percussion choose instruments and pieces where they can have a single note or chord. (For more ideas see YAMSEN in Appendix 1.)

Where possible, encourage intensive musical interaction as described by Margaret Corke and Intensive Interaction (see the work of Melanie Nind and David Hewitt). These pupils could benefit from working with a Music Therapist. For details of all these see Appendix 1.

Music technology can be used especially if repeated from week to week in the same conditions (see the work of Phil Ellis in Appendix 1).

For pupils with dyslexia

These pupils may excel at music. Where they normally experience problems with reading, here they are on equal terms with everyone else. Remember, they can have right-left and up-down confusions. Reading music may not be a problem, but if it is, the teacher should move on quickly to alternatives, be it graphic or tablature type notations, or playing by ear. With very complex scores coloured highlighter pens and larger print may be useful.

Music may help them to develop better literacy skills with its use of sequencing and removal of pressure.

A music teacher – Diane Ditchfield writes:

My own interest in dyslexia had come about in 1984 in a small public school in the United Kingdom. I also taught English to a small class of pre-GCSE girls, many of whom had been diagnosed as dyslexic. At the time it seemed to me that the girls who were in the chapel choir were making better progress in English than those who were not, and I wondered if this was because choral training helps the syllables. *Music and Dyslexia: Opening New Doors* (Ed. T.R.Miles and John Westcombe) (see Appendix 1).

For pupils with dyspraxia

These pupils may have problems with the co-ordination needed to play an instrument (and even to sit still). Being in a choir may improve their concentration and sitting skills. Where possible, use Brain Gym type musical co-ordination games as warm ups, and explore the musical elements using techniques from the Dalcroze teaching method.

For pupils with dyscalculia

This may lead to difficulties in working with music on a score. The sense of odd and even and the ability to count within a time signature may prove difficult and ways will need to be found to accommodate this. The Kodály type approach will help many using a regular set of word patterns to interpret rhythm patterns and the slow incremental approach of introducing new ideas.

Pupils with physical difficulties

When regarding any pupil with a physical or sensory impairment it is essential to think of their musical ability and interests first and their impairment second.

You can no more make an assumption about a pupil with physical difficulties than about any other pupil in the class. It is possible that the pupil will need no more than enough space in the room to get through in a wheelchair. You must get to know the pupil and their musical abilities as quickly as possible so that you can provide the right equipment. It is essential for these pupils that you keep appropriate equipment under lock and key and in good working order, checked by the technician well before the lesson.

If time is not a problem you should familiarise yourself with the equipment, but realistically, given the demands of a busy working day, this may not be possible. This is something that the support assistant could take off your hands. The technology may be similar to what s/he is used to from other lessons. This could also be a good opportunity for paired work with another pupil. The paired pupil could be someone who is planning a career in music technology.

Obviously, the aim is for the pupil to control the technology themselves. This equipment will be very attractive to all the class and their interest should be encouraged but not to the extent that they take over.

Pupils with sensory impairment

Hearing impairment

Pupils who are deaf and hearing impaired *can* take part in music lessons. They are as likely as any other pupil to have a good sense of rhythm. It is less likely – but possible – that they can have a good sense of pitch, even perfect pitch.

They work well with drums and wooden sounds. They are also good at reading signing, a skill which prepares them well for reading and so graphic scores, Kodály hand signs and even western music notation.

In performing, these pupils can be good in group ensembles such as gamelan and steel pans where visual contact with the rest of the group is important. However, they may need to look at the instrument as they play which can create some problems with watching the band leader.

When listening to music live instruments are always better. When listening to electronic instruments and CDs use top quality amplification or headphones, avoid too much reverb, turn up the bass and place the speaker on a wooden floor or resonance boards near to the pupil.

There are benefits from the increased aural perception which music develops. This may be an increased awareness of vibrations in the body rather than hearing actual sounds. Some hearing impaired pupils may wish to go on to do GCSE, A Level and even degree level music.

For further information, see Appendix 1 for the Beethoven Fund and Music and the Deaf.

Visual impairment

For pupils who are blind or visually impaired sound is the most important feature of the world around them. As a result they will probably be able to sing in tune and have developed a facility for playing on at least one instrument by ear. Music is a natural subject for them to study.

> Sally Zimmerman in her book 'Instrumental Music' states: 'I think all pupils in mainstream schools who live predominantly in the world of sound rather than vision should take GCSE music, if only to have one straightforward subject to study.'

They will make the most of a music lesson if they are able to tape any music or instructions to work through after the lesson. Braille music can be used but it is very slow and requires one hand to be scanning over the page whilst the other plays.

Although they may be very musical they will not necessarily find remembering large quantities of music any easier than the rest of the group. They will need strategies for learning. Sudden loud sounds can be a real shock. Loud music needs a warning, either physical or verbal.

It is important to find out how much vision the pupil has, and what type and colour of notation and lighting suites them best. Many pupils with visual impairment have some sight – they may be able to cope with music which has been enlarged – however, doing this on a computer program will be better than a straight photocopy. The photocopy will enlarge both spaces and notes – this may make it awkward to read and takes up a lot of space when what is needed is clear large notes but not great gaps in between.

These pupils should be given the opportunity to learn virtually any instrument. The person teaching them may need to try out more tactile ways of explaining techniques, it not being possible to show the pupil. Or an instrument tactile clues to aid the location of key notes will be important (like the raised dot found on the number 5 of the telephone).

Computer programs which don't rely on a mouse, such as Cakewalk, can be used with a Screen Reader such as Jaws.

Savants

Very rarely, a pupil with visual impairment will show a great talent for music at an early age. These pupils are sometimes known as savants if their musical ability is in advance of their years and not matched in any other area of development. These pupils need to be allowed to develop their skills and need to be put in touch with teachers who can stretch them.

Multi-sensory impairment

These pupils will be both visually and hearing impaired, and one of these is likely to be worse than the other. The teacher will rely on the support assistant for guidance as to the best strategies. Combinations of the methods above will work best. Vibro-tactile approaches will work well with these pupils. (For a list of vibro-tactile instruments see Appendix 1.)

Speech, language and communication difficulties

Semantic pragmatic disorder

Music is a means of communication which can unlock a pupil who is trapped without language. Whole sessions of music can be taught without having to speak. Pupils may understand sung instructions rather than spoken ones. In some instances, these pupils can sing even when they can't talk. Being able to play an instrument can harness their frustration, allowing them to express their emotions. This is the same for pupils who experience dysfluency, who may stammer or have difficulty pronouncing certain sounds.

Pupils with autism

These pupils may appear to be trapped within their own worlds and have no interaction with other people in school. To reach them the teacher must be familiar him/herself with Musical Interaction (see Appendix 1) or bring in a Music Therapist (see Appendix 1). Music is a vital way of learning to communicate with these pupils.

Pupils with Asperger's Syndrome

These pupils, just like the artistic pupil who has a fantastic eye for detail at one glance, may have an exceptional music talent. They may not like music, but if they do they may be obsessed with the detail and minutiae. There are two approaches: 1) go with the obsession and encourage its development; 2) redirect and avoid all contact with the obsession. It is probably best to discuss with the parents which they think is best for their child, and be prepared to change.

Cross-curricular themes

It is well known that learning music helps you learn just about everything else, and that it is a 'unique form of communication'. The music teacher will be familiar with the cross-curricular themes as detailed in the QCA National Curriculum document.

Music supports other subjects, skills and styles of learning, and especially with regard to pupils with SEN. It develops co-operative social skills and promotes self-esteem, so vital to those pupils with special needs, especially those with BESD.

Music supports learning in other subjects, and other subjects can support music, especially if departments agree to study related topics at the same time.

But music, in particular, has particular merits which support pupils with SEN:

1. Learning music develops cognitive skills

2. Learning to perform develops sequencing, and basic literacy and numeracy skills

3. All music involves counting, be it conscious or subconscious

4. Using a gong or sound beam develops spatial awareness

5. Singing reinforces language skills, including spelling

6. Songs' subject matter will give insight into any subject including: historical; geographical; cultural; spiritual etc.

7. Something to be learnt can be sung a hundred times, when a pupil would get bored of speaking it more than once.

8. Playing in an ensemble requires some social awareness and an ability to co-operate.

9. Music can seriously determine mood and can aid the control and concentration of pupils?

10. The pupils' own musical tastes offer a way into developing a relationship with them.

Summary

Music is a particularly suitable subject for pupils with special educational needs to learn. It is in itself a 'unique form of communication' and it also promotes learning in other subjects. It provides opportunities for success when other subjects seem to offer only difficulties. It may not always receive the recognition it deserves as a curriculum subject, but for many pupils it is the highlight of their week in school.

Appendices

Useful Contacts, Books and Articles

General contacts and associations

The National Curriculum for England and Wales
(Published by the DfES and QCA)
Available from:
HMSO
St Clement's House
2–16 Colegate
Norwich NR3 1BQ

National Association of Music Educators (NAME)
Administrator: Helen Fraser
NAME
Snitterton Road
Matlock
Derbyshire DE4 3LZ
www.name.org.uk

NAME brings out many publications each year which deal with subjects relevant
to the classroom music teacher.

National Association for Special Educational Needs (NASEN)
NASEN House
4/5 Amber Business Village
Amber Close
Amington
Tamworth B77 4RP
www.nasen.org.uk

National Music and Disability Information Service (NMDIS)
7 Tavern Street
Stowmarket IP14 1PJ
Tel: 01449 673990
www.directions-plus.org.uk; emil: info@directions-plus.org.uk

NMDIS seeks to enable disabled people to have the choice to enjoy, be involved
with, and to benefit from music. They work alongside Sound Sense, an organisation
which promotes community music, and have articles in their publications.

Kodály Society
Secretary: Judy Hildesley
31 Woodlands Road
London SW13 0JZ
Tel: 020 8876 0321
www.britishkodalyacademy.org; email: hildesley@aol.com

The Kodály Society organises workshops and summer schools promoting the Kodály method of music teaching, which is ideal for pupils with learning disabilities. The hand signs work well with deaf and hearing impaired pupils and even autistic pupils.

The Voices Foundation
38 Ebury Street
London SW1W 0LU
Tel: 020 7730 6677 Fax: 020 7259 0598
email: vf@voices.org.uk

The Voices Foundation runs courses for teachers explaining Kodály method and singing class techniques.

The Orff Society (UK)
7 Rothesay Avenue
Richmond
Surrey TW10 5EB
www.orff.co.uk

The Orff Society organises workshops and summer schools which promote the Orff method of teaching music. This method has many ideas which work well with pupils with disabilities.

The Dalcroze Society UK (Inc.)
100 Elborough Street
London SW18 5DL
Tel/Fax: 020 8870 1986
email: admin@dalcroze.org.uk; www.dalcroze.co.uk

The Dalcroze method promotes the use of movement to explore the elements of music. It is ideally suited to reaching pupils with learning disabilities. The society runs workshops and summer schools.

Rhythmics develops an understanding of musical elements such as pulse, tempo, rhythm, phrasing, duration and structure through movement. It explores all aspects of the relationship between music and movement, as well as that between creativity and technique.

Yorkshire Association for Music and Special Educational Needs (YAMSEN)
The West Park Centre
Spen Lane
Leeds LS19 7LL
www.yamsen.org.uk

A regional charity which organises events for pupils and adults with varying difficulties. Runs informal training workshops. Publishes the Earwiggo Books which have lots of basic ideas for music lessons with pupils who have learning difficulties.

Nicholas Haines Consultancy
Bank House
19/21 Church Street
Haxey
North Lincolnshive DN9 2Hy
Tel: 01427 753150; Fax: 01427 752209
email: sales@nicholashaines.com

Headphone Hospital; keyboard workstations

General books

Birkenshaw-Flemming, Lois (1989) *Come On Everybody Let's Sing*. Warner Chappell Music Canada Ltd. ISBN 0-769-29965-2.

Birkenshaw-Flemming, Lois *Music for Fun, Music for Learning*. Holt, Rinehart and Winston. ISBN 0-918812-23-2.

Two books which introduce material which works well with pupils of differing disabilities, particularly learning disabilities. The first contains information about working methods suitable for these pupils.

Ocarina Workshop Publications
PO Box 56
Kettering
Northants NN15 5LX
Tel: 01536 485963
www.ocarina.co.uk

The Ocarina Workshop supplies the instruments, publishes their own materials using their own graphic notation, and leads training days for teachers and workshops for children and adults.

For pupils with emotional, behavioural and social developmental needs

Foxwood Song Sheets
Available from YAMSEN (see above).

A system of deliberately imprecise notation.

Education Psychology Service
Derby City Education Service
Middleton House
27 St Mary's Gate
Derby DE1 3NN

Also available in an unpublished guide used by Derby City Education Service comprising 2 booklets: *Classroom Behaviour Management* and *Rules, Praise, Ignore*.

For pupils with learning disabilities

Wood, Miriam (1983) *Music for People with Learning Disabilties.* The Guernsey Press Ltd. ISBN 0-285-63155-1.

This book explores how to work with music and children and adults with learning disabilities, albeit in a special school type environment.

Exams for pupils with learning difficulties

Welsh Joint Education Committee
245 Western Avenue
Cardiff CF5 2YX
www.wjec.co.uk

WJEC Entry Level Certificates
The main features of the certificates are: (a) the provision of appropriately structured assessment programmes (b) specifications supported by stimulating and attractive resources (c) the active involvement of teachers as course producers, resource producers and assessors (d) the establishment of a feedback system for pupils and teachers and the encouragement of innovation in the delivery of the curriculum.

The specifications, resource materials, assessment techniques and reporting systems emphasise the positive and raise pupils' self-esteem. It is also a proven means of motivating many youngsters who may otherwise have turned their backs on education. Most specifications are also co-teachable with their GCSE equivalents and are developed to fit into the National Qualifications Framework.

For pupils with multisensory impairment, SLD and PMLD

Corke, Margaret (2002) *Approaches to Communication through Music.* London: David Fulton.

This book explores how to use music and intensive interaction for pupils with PMLD. It gives musical examples and case studies.

Hewitt, Dave and Nind, Melanie (2001) *A Practical Guide to Intensive Interaction.* BILD (British Institute for Learning Disabilities).

Nind, M. and Hewitt, D. (1998) *Interaction in Action.* London: David Fulton.

Nind, M. and Hewitt, D. (2003) *Access to Communiction: Developing the Basics of Communication for People with Severe Learning Difficulties.* London: David Fulton.

For pupils with multisensory impairment

Vibro-tactile instruments:
    Big Bomb
    Tone Bars
    Vibro-tactile Drum Tables
    Bass Drums
    Timpani

can be bought from:

LMS Music Supplies
PO Box 7
Exeter EX1 1WB
Tel: 01392 428108
www.lmsmusicsupplies.co.uk

Percussion plus suppliers of percussion instruments on fixed stands:

Soundabout
Ormerod School
Waynflete Road
Oxford OX3 8DD
Tel: 01865 744175; Fax: 01865 308916
email: info@soundabout.org.uk
website: www.soundabout.org.uk

Soundabout exists to help those people who have complex disabilities to develop their ability to communicate and interact with the world around them through music and sound. *Soundabout* runs workshops on the use of Resonance Boards and the Sound Beam for pupils with PMLD.

For pupils with physical disabilities

Drake Music Project Central Services
The Deptford Albany
Douglas Way
London SE8 4AG
www.drakemusicproject.com

The Drake Music Project has pioneered ways of exploring music composition and performance for children and adults with physical difficulties, using music technology.

Suppliers of specialist ICT equipment and switches

Quality Enabling Devices Ltd
1 Prince Alfred Street
Gosport PO12 1QH
www.qedltd.com

This company supplies switches and Quintet. They will give advice on the best switch solution for creating music.

The Soundbeam Project
Unit 3 Highbury Villas
Kingsdown
Bristol BS2 8BY
www.soundbeam.co.uk

This company gives demonstrations and advice about the use of the soundbeam as well as supplying the equipment.

CARESS
Creating Aesthetically Resonant Environments in Sound
School of Arts, Design and Media
Bede Tower
Ryhope Road
University of Sunderland SR2 7EG
phil.ellis@sunderland.ac.uk; www.bris.ac.uk/caress

Phil Ellis has researched the use of the Soundbeam with pupils who have PMLD. He has brought out videos which show this work.

MIDIcreator
York Electronics Centre
University of York
Heslington
York YO10 5DD
Tel: 01904 432323
Fax: 01904 432333
www.midicreator.com/contacts.html

For advice on MIDIcreator contact Mark Hildred at:

Immersive Media Spaces Ltd
Innovtion Centre
York Science Park
York YO10 5DS
Tel: 01904 561520
sales@immersive.com; www.immersivemediaspaces.co.uk

For pupils who are deaf and hearing impaired

The Beethoven Fund
2 Queenswood
London NW8 6RE

The Beethoven Fund encourages the development of resources, instruments and workshops for the hearing impaired. They work closely with Claus Bang (a teacher of music for the Deaf in Denmark) and Music and the Deaf.

Music and the Deaf
The Media Centre
7 Northumberland Street
Huddersfield HD1 1RL
www.matd.org.uk

Music and the Deaf, started by Paul Whittaker, offers workshops, after-school clubs and advice.

Publications

Music and the Deaf   *Key Stage 1, 2 & 3 Workbook*

Their newest publication is a course of work for Key Stage 3 researched over the last few years.

For blind and visually impaired

RNIB
105 Judd Street
London WC1H 9NE
www.rnib.org.uk

An advisory service and email conference is available which supports the work of music teachers working with pupils who are visually impaired.

Publications

Zimmerman, Sally-Anne (1998) *Instrumental Music*. London: RNIB. ISBN 1-85878-153-1.

A book explaining the problems a person without sight may experience when learning an instrument and the various methods of dealing with this.

Ockelford, Adam (1996) *Music Matters*. London: RNIB. ISBN 1-85878-071-3.

A useful explanation of the role of music in the life of a pupil who is blind or visually impaired, with detailed explanations of suitable notations, especially Braille notation.

For pupils with dyslexia and dyscalculia

Oglethorpe, Sheila (1996) *Instrumental Music for Dyslexics*. London: Whurr. ISBN 1-86156-291-8.

A discussion of the problems a dyslexic pupil may find when learning music – although from a piano teacher's point of view it contains information which is useful for the mainstream music teacher.

Miles, T. R. and Westcombe, J. (2001) *Music and Dyslexia*. London: Whurr. ISBN 1-86156-205-5

A collection of articles by people who are dyslexic, and their teachers, explaining their relationship with music and its effects on their lives/careers.

For pupils with dyspraxia

Brain Gym
Educational Kinesiology UK Foundation
12 Golders Rise
London NW4 2HR
Tel: 020 8202 3141
Fax: 020 8202 3890
email: brain.gymgb@euphony.net; www.braingym.org

This will give a list of tutors, courses and resources.

British Society of Music Therapists
61 Church Hill Road
East Barnet
Hertfordshire EN4 8SY
Tel: 020 8441 6226; Fax: 020 8441 4118
email: info@bsmt.org
www.bsmt.org.uk

The Society produces a journal with information about music therapy.

Nordoff, P. and Robbins, C. (1971) *Music Therapy in Special Education*. MMB Music Inc., ISBN 0-918812-22-4.

Nordoff, P. and Robbins, C. (1971) *Therapy in Music for Handicapped Children*. London: Gollancz.

Written in the 1970s when this was pioneering work, these books explore how important music can be for pupils with learning and other disabilities. They consider which instruments work best, the type of musical instruments to use, and the effects of the music on the children.

For further information about Music Therapy contact:
The Nordoff Robbins Centre Music Therapy Centre
2 Lissenden Gardens
London NW5 1PP
www.nordoff-robbins.org.uk

For pupils with Autism and Asperger's Syndrome contact:
Sutherland House School
Westward
68 Cyprus Road
Mapperley Park
Nottingham NG3 5ED

The school seeks to act as an information and continuing resource centre for all parents of children with autism and for professionals involved with them throughout the area, whether or not they attend the school. It is committed to working in partnership with other agencies.

Articles about music and autism

Levis, Rhian, Prevezer, Wendy and Spencer, Ruth *Musical Interaction: An Introduction.* Sutherland House School.

This very practical paper discusses the rationale behind musical interaction therapy and sets out clearly the ways it can be used in a school setting. The whole process is described so that teachers, speech therapists and parents can take from it ideas for adapting their own play interactively with the child, even where a music therapist is not available.

Prevezer, Wendy *Entering into Interaction*

This booklet was originally written for speech and language therapists, but is relevant to anyone working or living with a young child with autism. For use with children at a pre-verbal stage and those already using some language, with some reference to higher level language skills. It draws on ideas and strategies developed within 'Musical Interaction' sessions at Sutherland House School, but aims to make this way of working accessible to those in less specialised settings, without a musician. The emphasis is on detailed practical strategies for enabling communication, such as following the child (i.e. non-directive techniques), and using songs and musical games as frameworks.

What Do We Really Think?

Each member of the department should choose two of these statements and pin them on to the notice board for an overview of staff opinion. The person leading the session (Head of Department, SENCO, senior manager) should be ready to address any negative feedback and take forward the department in a positive approach.

- If my own pupil had special needs, I would want her/him to be in a mainstream school mixing with all sorts of kids.

- If my own daughter had Cerebral palsy, I would want her to stay in a small caring environment, not come to be 'included' in a massive high school, where she is at risk of being bullied or ridiculed by the so-called 'able-bodied'.

- I want to be able to cater for pupils with SEN but feel that I don't have the expertise required.

- Special Needs kids in mainstream schools are all right up to a point, but I didn't sign up for dealing with the more severe problems – they should be in special schools.

- It is the SENCO's responsibility to look out for these pupils with SEN – with help from support teachers.

- Pupils with special needs should be catered for the same as any others. Teachers can't pick and choose the pupils they want to teach.

- Research shows that pupils with MLD can't handle being in large classes. Can we alter class sizes, or otherwise make them feel comfortable?

- I need much more time to plan if pupils with SEN are going to be coming to my lessons.

- Big schools are just not the right places for blind or deaf kids, or those in wheelchairs.

- I would welcome more training on how to provide for pupils with SEN in music.

- I have enough to do without worrying about kids who can't read or write.

- If their behaviour distracts other pupils in any way, youngsters with SEN should be withdrawn from the class.

- I can see the point of avoiding 'sink groups' where students with behaviour difficulties never get a chance to see better-behaved kids in operation.

- Musical equipment is too expensive to let pupils with SEN loose with it.

- Music can be really valuable in giving opportunities to pupils with learning difficulties – opportunities that they don't get in other subjects.

Case Studies

1. Jed, Year 9 (Autistic Spectrum Disorder)

2. Janine, Year 7 (Hearing Impairment)

3. Dale, Year 10 (Moderate Learning Difficulties)

4. Julia, Year 9 (Visual Impairment)

5. Mandeep, Year 11 (PMLD)

6. Natashe, Year 8 (Dyslexia)

7. David, Year 10 (BESD)

1 Jed, Year 9 (Autistic Spectrum Disorder)

Jed is in Year 9 and is autistic. When he first came to the music lessons in the High school, Jed would run out of the room when anyone played a loud sound, or put his hands over his ears and scream. The teacher thought this was because the sounds were frightening him or that he had really sensitive hearing. After a term the teacher and the TA began to realise that he was fine in the lessons provided he was prepared for the sounds of some of the instruments such as the drum-kit and the trumpet. If this was done he would actually enjoy listening to them.

In order to help him, the TA started to use a PECS book (Picture Exchange Communication System): this has Velcro lines on each page, to which picture cards can be attached. The TA uses this to set out a timetable for Jed each day – some of the pictures are of an object of reference for the subject, some are a picture of the teacher. This is especially useful in preparing Jed for anything that is going to be different from the normal routine.

In music lessons, the TA has a supply of pictures of the instruments (made by using the school's digital camera) and shows these to Jed before they are played. He is now able to understand what will happen next and can remain calm. Jed is also able to point to the picture of the instrument he would like to play and exchange the picture for the instrument.

By the end of Year 8 Jed would not just tolerate the loudest of the instruments, but actually seemed to enjoy them.

Much of the time Jed didn't appear to be paying any attention in lessons, but the TA would sometimes catch him singing part of a song they had learned three or four weeks before. She started to keep a diary of these occurrences and realised that he had in fact been taking in much of the lesson content.

If the lesson was based around rhythm notation Jed could always clap the rhythm straight away, and if he listened to a melody on the keyboard he was able to repeat it without any mistakes, often after only one hearing. The teacher and TA were only able to discover this when they had put in strategies to calm him down, thus it took a long time to understand the extent of his abilities. He could still be disturbed or found not concentrating during the lessons, but by now the staff were more confident of finding ways to help him.

The teacher is now considering entering Jed for GCSE music and has designed a programme for him which works well alongside all the other pupils in the class. This consists of rhythm work using notation, playing basic tunes on the keyboard for him to copy, playing chords on chime bars, and then transferring these to the keyboard using Foxwood song sheets (see Appendix 1). Jed has directed a group of pupils when to play and when to stop.

2 Janine, Year 7 (Hearing Impaired)

Janine is in Year 7 and has a Cochlea Implant. She communicates using a mixture of speech and sign language.

She enjoys music lessons and is hoping to be able to learn the cello with a peripatetic teacher who visits the school.

The music teacher has always encouraged Janine to join in the music lessons. This has resulted in her doing a lot of basic percussion sessions which have enabled her to develop her good sense of rhythm. She particularly enjoyed playing the bass drum and the congas.

During a recent school production she was chosen to play the xylophone.

She found it quite easy to learn how to play the piece by watching the teacher demonstrate the piece and, understand where the pattern of notes was the same and where it changed. The teacher had been teaching form and had explained that the piece had the form ABAA; this understanding made it easier for Janine to play. She found that she needed to remember the piece because she needed to watch her hands as she played to make sure she had the correct notes – as she was not able to hear them all clearly (especially when the others were playing). Playing next to her friend helped. Although she learnt the notes quickly she found it hard when she had to maintain a steady pulse and to play the long notes the right length. She realised that she found the music easy to play when there was a note on every beat, but struggled with the longer notes, finding it hard to imagine the length of time needed for the minims and semibreves.

The music teacher suggested that Janine should try some country dancing. This was not easy; walking and dancing in time with all the other people proved very difficult and required a lot of concentration. However, by the end of the term she found she understood how to play better because of the dancing. The constant counting of eight and four beats had fixed the patterns in her mind and she was able to imagine the length of the long notes and understand the pattern of the four phrases ABAA better.

3 Dale, Year 10 (Moderate Learning Difficulties)

Dale is working towards the Welsh Board Entry level certificate.

The class are writing a song, concentrating on how to give the melody structure chords. They have listened as a group to a variety of songs from different cultures and have noted the form of these.

Many pupils in the class have already written several songs. The music teacher has written down a set of activities for the TA to work through with Dale over the next four weeks which will lead to him creating his own 16 bar piece.

1. Play the notes of the Pentatonic to get used to the sound. He uses a xylophone with the pentatonic scale CDEGA. The TA encourages him to play the notes for a while, letting him listen to the sounds. He doesn't do this for long,

2. Think of a subject and create a short poem. The TA suggests that he tries to think of some words which he would like to use. He finds this easy, and lists his favourite friends. He is able to use this idea to say several lines which the TA writes down as a four line stanza.

3. Clap the rhythm of the words you've written; together the TA and Dale clap this many times. Dale does not find this easy. The TA gets a drum and he enjoys this more – although it is quite difficult. They try Claves – he finds this easier and starts to be able to play the pattern.

4. Using the notes of the pentatonic create your first line A. Dale plays on the instrument again, finding a pattern that he likes. The TA writes this down as melody using letter names. They record the sounds as he goes along onto a tape recorder.

5. Find a different set of notes for line B. Dale experiments and then settles on a group of notes he likes. He notes it down as B, writing down the letter names. They record it.

6. Put your ideas together in the form AABA. They use the two tunes Dale has written in the pattern given. Dale is not sure about using the same tune three times, but the teacher reassures him that they sing many songs which do this – finding an example for him to listen to.

7. Either sing your tune yourself or ask a friend to do it for you onto the tape. Dale wants to sing the song. He has been listening to the tape of the song at home and is really happy to perform it through a Microphone for the rest of the class. The teacher plays the tune. They record it.

8. Add chords to this. This is too difficult for Dale, but he is happy to hear his tune played with the chords added by the teacher. She marks these in for him in large letters, and then asks two other pupils to come and accompany Dale on the guitar and drums. The teacher is able to record this as a piece which Dale has composed (noting the part played by herself and the TA), and can also use this as an ensemble performance.

4 Julia, Year 9 (Visual Impairment)

Julia has private lessons at home on the piano and on the flute.

Although she loves her school she finds the music lessons quite difficult.

The teacher has asked the class to write a song, working with partners. Julia is sharing a keyboard with her best friend, Alice. They each have headphones so that they can work together on the piece; Julia finds them difficult and uncomfortable but if she takes them off she can't concentrate because of all the other noises in the classroom.

Her friend is writing down the tune, and Julia is recording any good musical ideas on her own personal mini disk recorder.

They are both trying to think of words for the piece.

Eventually, Julia decides she will finish the tune at home and asks Alice to do the words.

In the next lesson, the teacher realises that Julia is finding it difficult to work with the headphones on and allows Julia and Alice to work in a practice room. They then get on really quickly and produce a really good song which Alice is going to sing, with Julia playing the accompaniment.

They perform it in the summer concert.

They spend two music lessons practising the piece on the concert stage, and Alice helps the TA put chairs and music stands out as if the orchestra and the other players are there. As a result, on the concert night Julia is able to move reasonably confidently to her playing position only minimally guided by Alice.

In order to create a really good ensemble and avoiding counting aloud to start, Julia has added an introduction. She starts the piece when the concert hall is really quiet, with Alice joining in at the appropriate time.

5 Mandeep, Year 11 (PMLD)

Mandeep is operating at P level 3.

P3 (i) Pupils begin to communicate intentionally. They seek attention through eye contact, gesture or action. They request events or activities, for example, leading an adult to the CD player. They participate in shared activities with less support. They sustain concentration for short periods. They explore materials in increasingly complex ways, for example, tapping piano keys gently and with more vigor. They observe the results of their own actions with interest, for example, listening intently when moving across and through a Soundbeam. They remember learned responses over more extended periods, for example, recalling movements associated with a particular song from week to week.

P3 (ii) Pupils use emerging conventional communication. They greet known people and may initiate interactions and activities, for example, performing an action such as clapping hands to initiate a particular song. They can remember learned responses over increasing periods of time and may anticipate known events, for example, a loud sound at a particular point in a piece of music. They may respond to options and choices with actions or gestures, for example, choosing a shaker in a rhythm band activity. They actively explore objects and events for more extended periods, for example, tapping, stroking, rubbing or shaking an instrument to produce various effects. They apply potential solutions systematically to problems, for example, indicating by eye contact or gesture the pupil whose turn it is to play in a 'call and response' activity.

Mandeep is greatly motivated by music so he was allowed to choose to be in the GCSE Music class as an option at the end of Year 9. He can blink when he has a preference for something, and is able to control the movement of his feet to activate a Soundbeam. The school bought a Soundbeam system to add to their existing music equipment which included Cubase running on two work stations and a class set of 15 keyboards. The music teacher and the TA were sent on a day course to learn how to use the Soundbeam.

(www.soundbeam.co.uk)

The class are composing a piece for an occasion.

Mandeep's lessons over the 6 weeks

Session 1

The class hear examples of music for occasions, (Walton's *Te Deum* used for the Coronation of Elizabeth 2). Mandeep found the sudden loud outbursts in this music difficult to cope with at times, and had reflex reactions to the high volume, flinging his arms out and knocking someone on the head.

The second time he heard this he coped better: the teacher turned the music down a little and warned the TA when the music was about to start so that she could prepared Mandeep for the sound.

Other ceremonial pieces by Handel and Purcell were played. Mandeep was able to listen to these pieces as well as anyone in the group. The teacher realised that any sudden outbursts in the music (which are features of these pieces) may lead to a sudden reflex reaction, but that this did not mean that Mandeep was not enjoying the music. She ceased to worry about this – just making sure that neither he nor anyone else came to any harm.

A discussion ensued as to the nature of these pieces, the use of certain instruments to give them their character. The teacher played short extracts again and got two members of the group to play the relevant instruments, trumpet and trombone, making sure to warn Mandeep that this would happen. During this discussion the technician or TA was able to set up the Soundbeam ready for the next part of the lesson.

The whole group was split into small groups and set the task of exploring ways to open their own piece of music in a suitably dramatic way. Some went out to practice rooms. The Soundbeam was set up in a practice room, and Mandeep, with another two students, Claire and James, was able to work in there. Each sound on the sound module, which the Soundbeam has access to, has a set of brightly coloured A4 laminated pictures to enable Mandeep to chose the sound he likes, some being pictures of instruments and some being the object making a sound effect. Mandeep finds these hard to see and lets them know which sound he likes in his own way which they have learned to interpret.

The beam was set up so that any deliberate movement of Mandeep's foot was picked up, and so he could move his foot in front of the beam indicating when he likes a sound. This took the rest of the lesson. He seemed to prefer the really loud sounds, possibly not hearing the really quiet ones. The other two pupils did the same on the keyboard, finding sounds and rhythm patterns. They discussed how to write this piece – what they will need to write down, how they will do this, how they will use the Soundbeam as part of the piece.

Having chosen a sound, in agreement with the other pupil they change the other parameters – number of notes in the beam, length of the beam, type of scale, and pitch. The other two pupils took part in this and together they then found complementary sounds on their keyboard. They were choosing their own sounds and making up short tunes with single finger chords. Mandeep listened to what they were doing and would play the beam when he chose to.

Sessions 2–3

Over the next 2 sessions Mandeep developed ways of playing the beam at a signal from the other pupils.

Session 4

After three weeks Claire and James had written a grid plan of which sounds would be played and when, with a simple finger chord plan along the bottom of the grid. They have decided to add in some untuned percussion for dramatic effect.

With guidance from the teacher they decide that it would be best to record Mandeep's soundbeam music through the computer. They find that this makes it easier for them to play alongside his music, and to actually notate this part of the music.

Mandeep is able to activate this music using a switch. The places where they want this to happen are written into the grid.

Session 6

By week six the students are ready to put the various sections of the piece together and record it onto tape. Mandeep triggers the sounds he created using a switch linked to the computer, with Claire playing a tune with single finger chord accompaniment on the keyboard and James adding in large cymbal crashes at the end. The TA prepares Mandeep for these so that they don't make him jump.

6 Natasha, Year 8 (Dyslexia)

Natasha finds that she is very good at music and enjoys playing the piano by ear and singing almost every advert on the television. However, since coming into Year 8, she has begun to dread her music lessons.

At the beginning of the term the new teacher informed the class that she wanted them all to be able to read music by the end of the year. In fact, many of the pupils have private lessons and have been reading music for many years. Natasha doesn't tell her friends how much she enjoys playing the piano in case they ask her to sight read a new tune. She is very worried about the new teacher's plan and starts to sit at the back of the classroom and sometimes gets into trouble for messing about.

The teacher has realised that although there are many in the class who read music easily, there are some for whom it is going to be really difficult. She is aware that Natasha is dyslexic, but is not sure how this will affect her music making.

In order to put all the class on a level playing field she decides to teach them all to read Tonic sol fah using the Kodály method which she had learned on a Voices Foundation Course. This system uses hand signs to indicate relative pitch (see p.63). There is a sign for each note of the major scale.

Natasha cannot believe it when she finds that she does not have to look at small dots on lines. (In the past when she had tried this they often appeared to move about, and she found it very difficult to follow a line all the way across the page – she heard that this was called a 'mid line flick'.) She also finds that because she has spent a lot of time listening to the notes and playing by ear she is very good at this method of 'reading music'. She decides that she would like to sit at the front of the class now.

By the end of the year she can read a whole song from the signs. The teacher has fulfilled her aim as all the rest of the class have discovered this different way of reading music.

7 David, Year 10 (BESD)

David has a statement for BESD. He also has very poor handwriting skills and, having been excluded from school several times, he has missed whole chunks of his education. He is embarrassed about his writing and tries to do as little as possible. He has his own drum-kit at home and plays for the local youth club rock band.

Although he loves playing drum-kit he hates all other musical activities, and habitually engages in low level violence against other pupils. He also upsets the other pupils with inappropriate remarks about sex. He is frequently in the referral/inclusion room where he is sent for infringing the classroom rules.

Playing drum-kit is the one place where David is better than most other pupils. His self-esteem demonstrably rises when he is performing in class, to the school or just to the peripatetic drum-kit teacher, with who he has a good relationship. He loves other people knowing how good he is, and frequently asks if he is better than Catriona, the school's other top drummer (they are roughly the same standard).

When he is playing drum-kit at concerts outside school he always tries his best. Sometimes at rehearsals he sulks and ruins it for the school's jazz/rock band. Then he may choose not to come to rehearsals for weeks on end.

The music teacher and the SENCO have negotiated with the Head of Year that, whatever David has done, his peripatetic lesson is an entitlement that he should never miss. Whenever his language or behaviour becomes unacceptable, the music teacher confines herself to a brief, 'less of the bad language, David', and goes on to praise somebody else's work, making sure that David hears her do it.

David is unlikely to get a good grade for GCSE as he has no interest in the listening and composing elements of the exam. But the music teacher thinks she may motivate him by broadening his experience of other live music. He could not sit still or keep quiet when she took the class to the local operatic society's version of 'Carmen', but the teacher had anticipated this and had a school mentor with her, who took David home early. (The mentor told David that she couldn't stay till the end, and would he like a lift early as she lived near.)

Next day he talked a lot about the opera, which was quite outside his normal experience. The music teacher continues to look for other musical events, such as local carnivals and 'battle of the bands' where he can broaden his listening experience and participate as a member of the audience and not as the 'star'. He is taking the Rock School drum-kit exams with the peripatetic drum teacher who is also trying to develop other percussion skills (e.g. timbale and congas). The teacher gets him to work with Catriona in a friendly and competitive way, and has negotiated with other subject teachers that sometimes he may 'cool off' in the music room. For David, music and drumming is a personal lifeline.

An Outline Policy for SEN Provision in the Music Department

General Statement

Example

> All members of the department will ensure that the needs of all pupils with SEN are met, according to the aims of the school and its SEN policy.

Definition of SEN

Example:

Cognition and Learning Needs	Behaviour, Emotional and Social Development Needs	Communication and Interaction Needs	Sensory and/ or Physical Needs
Specific Learning Difficulties (SpLD)	Behaviour, Emotional and Social Difficulties (BESD)	Speech, Language and Communication Needs	Hearing impairment (HI)
Dyslexia	Attention Deficit Disorder (ADD)	Autistic Spectrum Disorder (ASD)	Visual impairment (VI)
Moderate Learning Difficulties (MLD)	Attention Deficit Hyperactivity Disorder (ADHD)	Asperger's Syndrome	Multi-sensory impairment (MSI)
Severe Learning Difficulties (SLD)			Physical difficulties (PD)
Profound and Multiple Learning Difficulties (PMLD)			OTHER

Provision for staff within the Department

Example

The member of staff with responsibility for overseeing the provision of SEN within the department will attend liaison meetings and feedback to other members of the department. He will maintain the department's SEN information file, attend appropriate training and disseminate this to all departmental staff. All information will be treated with confidentiality.

Provision for pupils with SEN

Example

The pupils are taught in their tutor groups as music and the arts provide particular opportunities for pupils in their social development.

Pupils with SEN may receive additional support if they have a statement of SEN, are at School Action Plus or School Action. The staff in the music department will aim to support the pupils to achieve their targets as specified on their IEPs and will provide feedback for IEP or Statement reviews. Pupils with SEN will be included in the departmental monitoring system used for all pupils. Additional support will be requested as appropriate.

Resources and Learning Materials

Example

The department will provide suitably differentiated materials and, where appropriate, specialist resources for pupils with SEN. Support staff will be provided with curriculum information in advance of lessons and will also be involved in lesson planning. A list of resources is available in the department handbook and on the notice board.

Instruments and equipment will be tailored to each pupil's needs.

Staff Qualifications and Continuing Professional Development Needs

Example

A record of training undertaken, specialist skills and training required will be kept in the department handbook. Requests for training will be considered in line with the department and school improvement plan.

Monitoring and reviewing the policy

Example

The Department SEN policy will be monitored by the Head of Faculty on a planned annual basis, with advice being sought from the SENCO as part of a three yearly review process.

Inclusive Music Room Rules

1. Keep the room tidy, with a clear pathway for everyone to move around easily; bags and coats placed out of the way.

2. Play only the instruments assigned to you, when they are assigned to you. Take turns on drum-kits/piano etc.

3. Take care not to 'drown out' other people when practising.

4. Always tidy away instruments and equipment at the end of the lesson: leave drum-kits set up as they are.

5. Be quiet during the listening sessions.

6. Respect each other's musical tastes and opinions.

Music Questionnaire

Pupils can interview each other in pairs

Name of interviewer
Name of person interviewed
What musical equipment and/or instruments do you own?
What does music do for you?
Where do you listen to music? How often do you listen to music?
What are your favourite bands, musicians and types of music?
What difficulties do you have either listening to or playing music?

Possible answers: jogging, doing homework, minidisk-player, television, helps me concentrate, classical, hip-hop, rock, radio, mobile phone, every day, poor acoustics in practice room, not enough music in Braille for me, proper size keyboard won't fit on my wheelchair table, my mum laughs at my CDs, the baby cries all night, helps me sleep

Individual Behaviour Plan

Pupil *A Somebody*	DOB *11/ 1/1993*
Form *9JP*	

IBP NO *10* Start Date *9/9/06*	Review Date *11/11/06*

Concerns
Poor Behaviour

Details
- *Arrives late for lessons*
- *Disruptive behaviour in class*
- *Reluctant to follow instructions*
- *Does very little work in class*

Targets to be achieved in music lessons	Achieved	
	Yes	No
1 Arrives on time for lessons		
2 Completes the tasks set		
3 Allows other pupils to get on with their work		

Strategies
- Regular home contact
- In-class support
- Praise for good behaviour
- Encourage to attend the drummers' club on Thursdays

Staff	
Key Worker *A Person*	
LS Co-ordinator *A A Person*	

Monitoring and Assessment
- Daily Target Cards
- Half Term reviews

Inclusive Checklist for TAs in Music

MUSIC: Performing, Composing, Listening with pupils who have behaviour difficulties

Instruments and equipment *Do* ● Let pupil have free choice of instrument, but take care with delicate equipment ● Make sure loud instruments are not played at top volume ● Ensure they know where all their music, plectrums, sticks and beaters are kept. ● Have a ready supply of pens and pencils for those who come without *Don't* ● Allow them to bully others off an instrument ● Let them dominate/disrupt the lesson	**Teaching methods** *Do* ● Give firm, clear instructions ● Stay with pupil until they have understood the task ● Frequently remind them of school and music room rules ● Demonstrate good listening skills yourself ● Put your fingers to your mouth to indicate silence *Don't* ● Give them too much choice or an over-flexible brief ● Talk at all while music is being played, even to reply to the pupil
Activities *Do* ● Use easy keys to start with (A on Guitar, C on keyboards etc.) ● Be very patient when introducing new ideas ● Manage seating arrangements appropriately (split up trouble makers, provide good role models) *Don't* ● Let pupils change instruments too often, i.e. just after they have started getting somewhere ● Let them wander off task	**Plenary** *Do* ● Give plenty of warning that the end of the lesson is coming and stay with them while they write up and/or record their performance *Don't* ● Take over responsibility for writing up the notes for pupils

Good Behaviour Management in Music

Do	Don't
Learn pupils' names	Muddle through with 'you boy' etc.
Tell them what the lesson's aim is, maybe also put the aim on display	Launch into the lesson with no explanation
Look to praise good behaviour – catch them being good	Describe aloud behaviour that you don't want to see
Explain the rules, and praise **honestly** (ideally at a rate of 30 praise statements to 5 criticisms per session)	Say 'well done' when it wasn't
Record work on tape, on paper, by video and photographs	Limit ways of recording success
Provide certificates – sometimes publicly awarded for work well done, help offered to peers etc.	Devalue rewards by over-using them
Leave tasks and materials for them to practise during the week	Abandon something that the pupils may have been looking forward to
Give students responsibilities to suit their needs and abilities	Force people into roles they can't handle
Speak to everybody separately at least once	Give all your attention to attention seeking, badly behaved pupils
Give them bits of theory as soon as they are ready	Overdo the theory at the expense of enjoyment and satisfaction
Have something ready to include late-comers without needing to speak to them	Pay any overt attention to late-comers
Entertain and impress them with your own instrument playing	Bore them or make them feel inadequate with your own playing
Tell support staff what you want them to do	Expect support staff to read your mind

Do	Don't
Keep the pace snappy and change task every 10–20 minutes	Spend too long on any one task
Reinforce and repeat	Move on too quickly
Pick up swiftly on bullying, racism etc, express disapproval, get on with music	Over-react to minor misdemeanours
Change direction of lesson if it seems appropriate	Get sidetracked by answering unrelated questions, however musical or fascinating which will hold up your lesson.
Ensure that each lesson includes a satisfying musical experience	Lose track of time
Have a series of sanctions that allow the pupils to 'start again' (e.g. a minute sitting out)	Make threats you can't or won't carry out
Own up if you make a mistake	Attempt to give the impression that you are infallible
Question everything	Assume anything
Get to know what sort of music pupils like, and respect their taste	Try to impose your own tastes on them
Be careful about how you refer to pupils' home lives	Assume they have two parents at home, have a computer, have a car
Remember you are there to empower them on their route to independence	Encourage pupils to be unnecessarily dependent

Foxwood Listening Worksheet

Name	Form

Title	Title
Classical 1	*World Music* 2

Instrument/s			Instrument/s		
	Heard it before?	Smiley face? ◯		Heard it before?	Smiley face? ◯

Title	Title
Theme/music/pop/classic 3	*Pop* 4

Instrument/s			Instrument/s		
	Heard it before?	Smiley face? ◯		Heard it before?	Smiley face? ◯

Tick or cross HEARD IT BEFORE?
Like it? ☺ Take it or leave it ☺ Don't like it ☹
Draw or write the names of instruments heard.

References

Booth, T., Ainscow, M., Black-Hawkins, K., Vaughan, M. and Shaw, L. (2000) *Index for Inclusion: Developing Learning and Participation in Schools.* Bristol: Centre for Studies in Inclusive Education.

Bsquared (www.bsquaredsen.co.uk).

Classics for Kids (www.classicsforkids.com).

Corke, M. (2002) *Approaches to Communication Through Music.* London: David Fulton.

DfES (2004) *Removing Barriers to Achievement: The Government's Strategy for SEN 2004.* London: DfES.

DfES (2001) Revised Code of Practice. London: DfES.

Miles, T.R. and Westcombe, J. (2001) *Music and Dyslexia, Opening New Doors.* London: Whurr.

Nind, M. and Hewitt, D. (1994) *Access to Communication.* London: David Fulton.

Ockleford, A. (1998) *Music Matters.* London: RNIB.

Ofsted (2003) *Special Educational Needs in the Mainstream.* London: Ofsted.

Oglethorpe, S. (1996) *Instrumental Music for Dyslexics.* London: Whurr.

Prevezer, W. (1998) *Entering into Interaction.* Nottingham Regional Society for Adults and Children with Autism.

Questions Dictionary of Music. Birmingham: Questions Publishing.

Stakes and Hornby (2000) *Meeting Special Needs in Mainstream Schools* (2nd edn). London: David Fulton.

Zimmerman, S. (1998). *Instrumental Music.* London: RNIB.